THE GOSPELS: A HISTORICAL & CULTURAL JOURNEY

Written by Jerry Pattengale, PhD.

...-89317-502-8

...useum of the Bible™, a publishing imprint of Global Publishing Partners, LLC,

...blisher have made every effort to ensure that the information in this
...press time and disclaim any liability to any party for any loss, damage,
...by errors or omissions, whether such errors or omissions result from
...r any other cause. Furthermore, any internet addresses (websites, blogs,
...s, or the like in this book are offered only as a resource. They are not
...e or imply an endorsement by the publisher.

...an. Used with Permission.

...(ESV) are from The ESV® Bible (The Holy Bible, English
...y Crossway, a publishing ministry of Good News Publishers.
...eserved.

...) are taken from the Holy Bible, King James Version, which

...re taken from the Holy Bible, New International
...978, 1984, 2011 by Biblica, Inc.™ Used by permission

THE GOSP

THE GOSPELS

A Historical & Cultural Journey

JERRY PATTENGALE

museum of the Bible

Contents

Foreword

Some of the world's most celebrated written works come in bunches. We refer to these in many ways such as trilogies, sequels, chronicles, or series. J. K. Rowling's *Harry Potter* and C. S. Lewis's *The Chronicles of Narnia* series drew millions of readers and various film adaptations. The same is true of J. R. R. Tolkien's *Lord of the Rings* and so many others.

However, easily surpassing all of these series combined, in any decade, and throughout printing history since the late 1400's, is a different series—the Gospels. For most of their history they've been part of the Christian Bible, comprising the New Testament's first four books. Unlike the works mentioned above, though, the Gospels are four different books with four different authors retelling the life of Jesus from unique perspectives. They were all written in the first century AD in ancient Israel and still are best sellers. But the works already mentioned, the story of Jesus's life has been adapted for television and film since the inception of the modern media, with a current series, *The Chosen*, breaking records with viewership.

In the Museum of the Bible's bestselling book, its co-authors said the following. I share it here because it's a rare occasion of having an Orthodox Jew and Evangelical Christian collaborating on such a topic:

> Christians see the Gospels (the first four books of the New Testament) as reliable accounts of the life and ministry of Jesus of Nazareth. Because of his recorded words and works, Christians believe Jesus to be the *Messiah* (the mighty deliverer/king) promised by the Old Testament prophets. They see the book of Acts as the story of the birth and growth of the church, the Epistles (letters) as instructions for the people of God,

> and the book of Revelation as a prophecy about the end of this present age.[1]

The Early Church began to put these books in the front of its New Testament collection. After all, they contained the essence of the life of Jesus and his teachings. The Church leaders then and now realize the importance of these four books—which helps us to understand the modern phrase "It's the gospel truth!" The following book helps you to understand the historical and cultural nature of the story told in the four Gospels and the manifestation of this idiom in efforts to understand the magnitude of influence these books have had on society.

Robert (Bobby) Duke, Ph.D.
Chief Curatorial Officer
Museum of the Bible, Washington, DC

[1]Lawrence Schiffman and Jerry Pattengale, *The World's Greatest Book: The Story of How the Bible Came to Be*, 2nd ed. (Carol Stream, IL: Tyndale House Publishing, 2024), 7.

INTRODUCTION

The life of Jesus of Nazareth has shaped the course of human history more than any other figure. His teachings, actions, and ultimate sacrifice have inspired faith, provoked thought, and transformed lives across centuries and continents. But beyond the theological doctrines and religious traditions, there lies a deeply human story—one grounded in specific places, shaped by culture and conflict, and lived out through ordinary moments and extraordinary encounters.

This book offers a journey through the major moments of the Gospels, drawn from the four canonical accounts—Matthew, Mark, Luke, and John—and framed by the events that defined Jesus's public life. Each chapter focuses on a pivotal scene from his birth and baptism, through his ministry and miracles, to his death, resurrection, and final charge to his followers. The selected Scripture verses are drawn from three translations: the King James Version (KJV), the New International Version (NIV), and the English Standard Version (ESV), and the reflections provide historical and cultural background to deepen understanding of each passage.

Rather than a devotional or commentary, this collection serves as a narrative companion and is designed to be accessible, thoughtful, and reverent. It is not meant to persuade or preach, but to present—to offer a view into the world in which Jesus lived and to illuminate the meaning behind the moments that shaped the gospel story.

Whether you are encountering these stories for the first time or returning to them with fresh eyes, may this book bring clarity to the context, richness to the reading, and wonder to the witness of a life that continues to speak across time.

THE BIRTH & PREPARATION OF JESUS

THE ANNUNCIATION

Luke 1:26–38

Annunciation, Leonardo da Vinci, ca. 1472–1475. Uffizi Gallery, Florence, Italy.

AND IN THE SIXTH MONTH
THE ANGEL GABRIEL
WAS SENT FROM GOD
UNTO A CITY OF GALILEE,
NAMED NAZARETH,
TO A VIRGIN ESPOUSED TO A MAN
WHOSE NAME WAS JOSEPH,
OF THE HOUSE OF DAVID;
AND THE VIRGIN'S NAME
WAS MARY.

LUKE 1:26–27, KJV

The Annunciation, or announcement of Jesus's birth, took place in Nazareth, a small and obscure village in Galilee with a population of only a few hundred people. Mary's situation was precarious—an unmarried Jewish woman who became pregnant risked public shame, excommunication, or even death under the law. The angel Gabriel, whose name means "God Is My Strength," delivered a message that Mary would conceive by supernatural means and give birth to the Messiah.

For centuries, the Hebrew prophets spoke of a time when God would restore the glory of Israel, defeat her enemies, and bring peace to the world. It would be a glorious new age, ushered in by the Messiah (Hebrew for "anointed one") from the line of King David. Could this long-awaited time finally be at hand?

Nazareth, a modest village dependent upon the local agricultural business, was situated near the major trade routes of the Roman Empire, exposing its residents to different cultures. Jesus would become known as "Jesus of Nazareth" or simply as "the Nazarene." Matthew's Gospel points to this as the fulfillment of an Old Testament prophecy: "that he would be called a Nazarene" (Matthew 2:23, NIV).

The Archangel Gabriel, Masolino da Panicale, ca. 1430. National Gallery of Art, Washington, DC, USA.

The town, however, was not mentioned in the Hebrew Bible (Old Testament). One possible reason is that Matthew was not referring to a single prediction, but to a whole body of prophetic thought and writings about the Jewish Messiah. Some scholars believe that Nazarene, meaning "from Nazareth," is derived from *netser*, the Hebrew word for "branch." *Netser* was one of the names given to the future Messiah: "A shoot will come up from the stump of Jesse; from his roots, a Branch will bear fruit" (Isaiah 11:1, NIV), speaking of a descendant of King David. Today, the main word in Hebrew for Christians comes from the Hebrew word for the local people from Nazareth, *Notzrim* or Nazarenes.

The angel's instruction to Mary, that her baby would be called *Yeshua* (or Jesus), meaning "God Is Salvation," mirrored what the angel declared to her

The Prophecy of Isaiah, Francisco Bayeu, ca. 1778–1779. Museo Nacional del Prado, Madrid, Spain.

betrothed, Joseph, as recorded in Matthew, which noted "for he will save his people from their sins" (Matthew 1:21, ESV).

Mary's acceptance of this role put her in a precarious situation. At the very least, she might face rejection from her fiancé and ostracism from her peers and neighbors. Luke portrayed this young woman as responding to her situation in one of the most beautiful passages in the New Testament known today as the Magnificat (Latin for "magnifies," from Mary's first words). Mary recalled the great things God has done for the Jewish people, and she rejoiced in the privilege of being chosen to give birth to the long-awaited Messiah (see Luke 1:46–55). It is no wonder that, despite the risks, the Annunciation made Mary one of the most revered figures in Christianity, honored as a model of faith and obedience.

BEHOLD,
A VIRGIN SHALL CONCEIVE,
AND BEAR A SON,
AND SHALL CALL HIS NAME
IMMANUEL.

ISAIAH 7:14, KJV

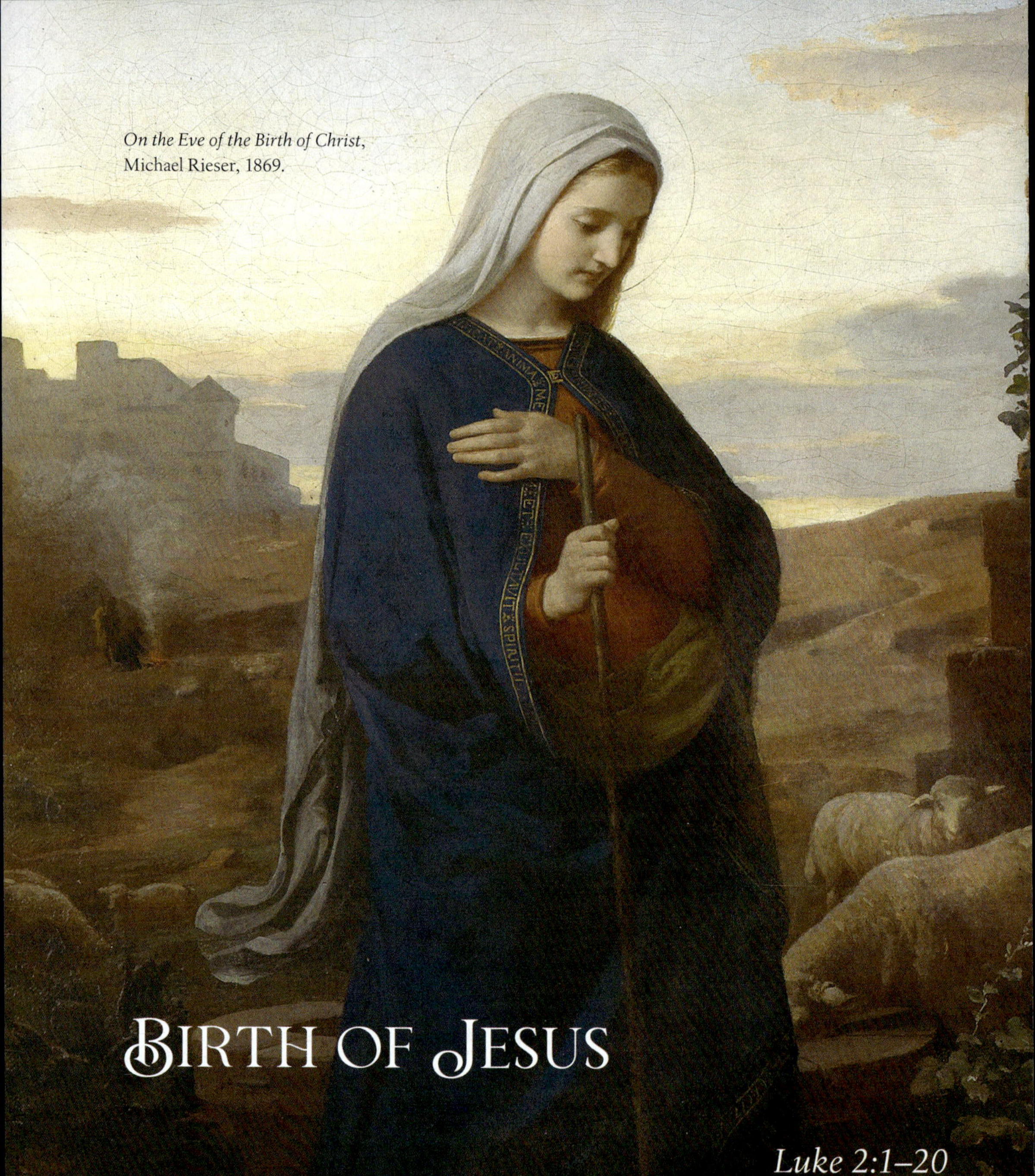

On the Eve of the Birth of Christ,
Michael Rieser, 1869.

Birth of Jesus

Luke 2:1–20

IN THOSE DAYS
CAESAR AUGUSTUS
ISSUED A DECREE
THAT A CENSUS
SHOULD BE TAKEN OF
THE ENTIRE ROMAN WORLD.

LUKE 2:1, NIV

Jesus was born under Roman rule during a time of significant political tension for the Jewish people. Roman Emperor Caesar Augustus declared that a census be taken of all people throughout the Roman world for taxation purposes. The Jewish people had been under Roman control since 63 BC, when Pompey invaded and captured Jerusalem. King Herod the Great had been appointed by Rome to govern the Jewish people living in their ancestral lands. Roman taxation was already a heavy burden on Jewish families, but the census was an even greater burden because it required everyone to register in their ancestral towns, even if they did not currently live there.

For Joseph and Mary, this meant traveling from Nazareth in the north 95 miles south to Bethlehem. Long before the creation of cars, the pair likely traveled on foot or possibly with a donkey. It would have taken them at least a week following the most popular route to reach their destination. This arduous journey would have been particularly difficult for a pregnant woman in her final trimester.

Adoration of the Child, Gerard van Honthorst, ca. 1620. Uffizi Gallery, Florence, Italy.

Bethlehem, historically associated with King David, was a small town just south of Jerusalem that became significantly overcrowded due to the census. Everyone in the ancestral line of David had to appear in this small town to register with the Roman government. So when Joseph and Mary arrived after a very long dusty and exhausting journey, they found no available lodging for travelers. The couple was forced to stay in a stable, most likely a grotto or exposed cave, which were often used as shelters for animals.

It was there, in that unglamourous forgotten place, that Jesus was born. His parents wrapped the baby boy in strips of cloth they either brought with them or borrowed from kindly villagers. And they laid their tiny newborn in a feed trough, possibly carved from stone, instead of a crib or regular bed.

Adoration of the Shepherds, Giorgione, ca. 1505–1510. National Gallery of Art, Washington, DC, USA.

Luke reported that local shepherds heard of this unusual birth. According to Mosaic Law, only unblemished lambs could be used for Temple sacrifices, and the lambs outside of Jerusalem were likely considered *migdal eder* (Hebrew, meaning "tower of the flock")—the best of the best. These special sheep were raised and shepherded by Levitical priests in the hills of Bethlehem and were by far the most valuable lambs in the country. It was these shepherds who were given the honor of being the first to visit Mary's infant son.

The nativity is often depicted as a peaceful pastoral scene, but, in reality, it was a moment of hardship and danger set against a backdrop of social, economic, and political unrest. Yet, through it, Jesus's humble beginnings were established, demonstrating his connection to common people and foreshadowing his teachings on justice, mercy, and the kingdom of God.

SHE BROUGHT FORTH
HER FIRSTBORN SON,
AND WRAPPED HIM IN
SWADDLING CLOTHES, AND
LAID HIM IN A MANGER;
BECAUSE THERE WAS NO ROOM
FOR THEM IN THE INN.

LUKE 2:7, KJV

The Adoration of the Magi, Edward Burne-Jones, 1904. Musée d'Orsay, Paris, France.

Visit of the Magi

Matthew 2:1–12

MAGI FROM THE EAST CAME TO JERUSALEM AND ASKED, "WHERE IS THE ONE WHO HAS BEEN BORN KING OF THE JEWS?"

MATTHEW 2:1-2, NIV

Although it was humble, the birth of Jesus did not go unnoticed by the scholars and political leadership of the time. A significant celestial event was observed by magi, also known as wise men, who were likely Persian or Babylonian scholars who practiced astrology, astronomy, and other forms of divination. The term *magi* comes from the Greek *magoi*, which referred to a class of priestly figures in Persia who were well-versed in interpreting celestial events.

In ancient times, celestial events were often interpreted as omens. What is often called the star of Bethlehem is the subject of much speculation today. Some scholars believe that the star could have been a supernova, a comet, or a rare planetary conjunction, such as the triple conjunction of Jupiter and Saturn in 7 BC.

Although we do not know the origins of the celestial event that transpired, it was significant enough to motivate the magi to act. Upon seeing it, they traveled westward on a long and arduous journey, likely along the ancient trade

Boswellia sacra, from which frankincense, a resinous dried sap, is harvested. Near Salalah, Oman. Photo credit: alexeys.

routes from Persia or Babylon that had long linked these empires with Jewish communities. Their quest potentially spanned several months.

Once they reached Jerusalem, the magi naturally assumed a newborn Jewish king would be found in the royal palace. Instead, they found Herod the Great, the paranoid Jewish ruler known for his brutal rule. Herod feared the prophecy of a new "king of the Jews," a title he had been given by Caesar, and saw it as a direct threat to his power. When his advisers pointed to the Hebrew book of Micah (Micah 5:2), which predicted that the Messiah would be born in Bethlehem, Herod instructed the magi to find the child and report back, though his true intention was to eliminate any potential threat to his throne.

The magi heeded the advice and followed the star to Bethlehem where they found Jesus, Mary, and Joseph. Overjoyed at finding the object of their search, the travelers presented Jesus with gifts of gold, frankincense, and myrrh. These gifts carried both practical and symbolic meaning. Gold represented kingship; frankincense—a Boswellia tree resin often burned as incense

Flight into Egypt, Eugène Girardet, ca. 1853–1907.

in worship—symbolized divinity; and myrrh—a Commiphora tree resin often used in perfumes and burials—symbolized sacrifice. All these gifts were precious commodities and would have been welcomed by the family.

After presenting their gifts, the magi were warned in a dream not to return to Herod. Instead, they returned home by another route. Sometime after the magi's visit, Joseph was also warned in a dream to flee to Egypt to escape King Herod's massacre of infants, later known as the Slaughter of the Innocents. Egypt was a natural place of refuge for the family, as it had a large and established Jewish community where the trio could find safety until Herod's death. These acts of defiance and self-preservation illustrate the political tensions and very real danger at the time of Jesus's birth.

WHEN THEY HAD OPENED THEIR TREASURES, THEY PRESENTED UNTO HIM GIFTS; GOLD, AND FRANKINCENSE AND MYRRH.

MATTHEW 2:11, KJV

Presentation in the Temple

Luke 2:21–38

The Presentation in the Temple,
Alvaro Pirez, ca. 1405–1415.
The Met Fifth Avenue, New York,
New York, USA.

AND WHEN THE DAYS OF
HER PURIFICATION ACCORDING
TO THE LAW OF MOSES
WERE ACCOMPLISHED,
THEY BROUGHT [JESUS] TO
JERUSALEM, TO PRESENT HIM TO
THE LORD.

LUKE 2:22, KJV

Unlike today, where names are officially recorded within minutes of birth, Jesus likely received his name at eight days old in the first of two ancient ceremonies. For thousands of years, Jewish boys have undergone the religious ritual of circumcision where they are also given their name. Jesus was given the name *Yeshua*, a derivative of Joshua, and rendered as Jesus in English. *Yeshua* is Hebrew for "God ('Yahweh') Is Salvation" or "God Saves" and is the name the angel Gabriel instructed both Mary and Joseph to give her son (Luke 1:31; Matthew 1:21).

Then just over a month after his birth, Mary and Joseph took Jesus to the Temple in Jerusalem to be consecrated to God as a firstborn son in accordance with Jewish law (Leviticus 12:1–8). This was a crucial act of Jewish identity and religious observance, because the law required that every firstborn male be dedicated to the Lord. The Temple itself was the center of Jewish worship. An immense and magnificent structure built by Herod the Great, it was one of the most impressive architectural feats of the ancient world, drawing pilgrims from all over the world to its outer courts which were accessible to everyone, while the inner sanctuaries were restricted.

Simeon the Righteous, Alexei Yegorovich Yegorov, ca. 1830–1840.

As part of her purification ritual, Mary offered a pair of doves or young pigeons, the offering permitted for people who could not afford a lamb (Leviticus 12:8). This highlights Mary and Joseph's modest financial status, reinforcing the reality of Jesus's humble beginnings.

Then the unexpected began to happen. Simeon, a devout elderly man who routinely waited in the Temple for the "consolation of Israel"—a phrase referring to the long-anticipated arrival of the Messiah—saw Jesus in the Temple that day. He then declared he had seen God's salvation, calling Jesus "a light to lighten the Gentiles, and the glory of thy people Israel" (Luke 2:29–32, KJV). This proclamation was radical and stunning in scope, suggesting that Jesus's mission was not only for Jews but also for Gentiles.

Nearby, Anna, an 84-year-old widow and prophetess who spent her days worshipping at the Temple, also saw Jesus. She quickly began praising God and speaking about him to other people who were waiting for the redemption of Jerusalem. The fact that both a man and a woman recognized Jesus's significance in the Temple reinforced the inclusivity of his mission.

These events also foreshadowed Jesus's future challenges. Although Simeon's blessing was joyous, his words to Mary were ominous: "A sword shall pierce through thy own soul also," predicting the suffering she would endure watching Jesus's crucifixion (Luke 2:35, KJV). Simeon's prophecy was the first clear indication of the painful sacrifice that awaited both Jesus and his family.

The Prophetess Anna, Rembrandt, 1639. Kunsthistorisches Museum, Vienna, Austria.

This moment at the Temple was the first recorded recognition of Jesus as the Messiah within the sacred heart of Judaism. It bridged the past prophecies with the future fulfillment of God's salvation plan, reinforcing how Jesus's life and mission were deeply tied to Jewish traditions.

FOR MY EYES HAVE SEEN YOUR SALVATION, WHICH YOU HAVE PREPARED IN THE SIGHT OF ALL NATIONS: A LIGHT FOR REVELATION TO THE GENTILES, AND THE GLORY OF YOUR PEOPLE ISRAEL.

LUKE 2:30–32, NIV

Jesus in the Temple as a Boy

Luke 2:41–52

Jesus Among the Doctors,
Jean-Auguste-Dominique Ingres, 1804.
Musée Ingres Bourdelle, Montauban, France.

AFTER THREE DAYS
THEY FOUND HIM IN
THE TEMPLE,
SITTING AMONG
THE TEACHERS,
LISTENING TO THEM
AND ASKING THEM QUESTIONS.

LUKE 2:46, ESV

Almost nothing is known about Jesus's youth except for one fascinating event to which many parents might relate: a lost child in a crowd. When he was twelve, Jesus and his family traveled to Jerusalem for Passover, one of the most important Jewish festivals, as they might have done every year of his life. The journey from Nazareth to Jerusalem was about 90 miles and took about a week to travel by foot. For safety, travelers made the journey in large caravans made up of family, friends, and neighbors. After days of dusty travel, the sight of Jerusalem's massive white-marble Temple would have been awe-inspiring to travelers arriving for the festival.

Jews traveled to Jerusalem to fulfill religious obligations as part of Passover's deeply significant commemoration of the Israelites' liberation from Egypt.

On Return from Jerusalem, It Is Noticed that Jesus Is Lost, James Tissot, ca. 1886–1894. Brooklyn Museum, Brooklyn, New York, USA.

Jewish families participated in the sacrificial rituals at the Temple, where thousands of worshippers brought unblemished lambs to be slaughtered. As the head of the household, Joseph would have performed the sacrifice for his family, and Jesus would have observed this moment that foreshadowed his own sacrificial role.

Passover was a weeklong festival, during which time Jesus and his family would have remained in Jerusalem. Some Jews may have celebrated for up to nine days to account for calendar inconsistencies. After the extended time away from their homes and several days' travel ahead of them, it's easy to imagine Joseph and Mary's focus on returning to Nazareth once the festival was complete. But after a day of travel during which time they believed Jesus was with friends or family in the returning caravan, they realized Jesus was not with them and swiftly returned to Jerusalem.

The biblical narrative records that after searching for three days, Joseph and Mary found Jesus in the Temple engaged in deep discussion with religious teachers. The Temple courts were known as a major center for theological study, and respected scholars commonly gathered to discuss interpretations of Jewish law. Their general astonishment at Jesus's wisdom and understanding suggests that, even at a young age, Jesus demonstrated a level of insight far beyond his years.

Jesus Found in the Temple, James Tissot, ca. 1886–1894. Brooklyn Museum, Brooklyn, New York, USA.

When Mary questioned Jesus about his disappearance, his reply was significant: "Didn't you know I had to be in my Father's house?" (Luke 2:49, NIV). It was a direct indication of his awareness of his divine mission. In Jewish culture, referring to God as "Father" in such a personal way was unusual and highlighted Jesus's unique relationship with God.

This surprising event is the only recorded story of Jesus's childhood and marks a key moment of transition from childhood to spiritual maturity. It sets the stage for Jesus's later public ministry, showing his early engagement with scripture and his growing awareness of his divine identity. The fact that he returned with his parents to Nazareth afterward, continuing to be obedient to them, underscores the balance between his divine calling and human upbringing. The narrative ends with a summary statement: "Jesus grew in wisdom and stature, and in favor with God and man" (Luke 2:52, NIV), emphasizing his development in intellect, physical growth, and spiritual favor.

EVERYONE
WHO HEARD HIM
WAS AMAZED
AT HIS UNDERSTANDING
AND HIS ANSWERS.

LUKE 2:47, NIV

Baptism of Jesus

Matthew 3:13–17

The Baptism of Christ, Joachim Patinir, ca. 1510. Kunsthistorisches Museum, Vienna, Austria.

THEN JESUS CAME
FROM GALILEE
TO THE JORDAN
TO BE BAPTIZED
BY JOHN.

MATTHEW 3:13, NIV

Jesus's baptism at the Jordan river by John the Baptist, marked the beginning of Jesus's public ministry. The Bible tells us that John and Jesus were related and close in age, with John being about half a year older. When the angel Gabriel told Mary that she would give birth to Jesus, he also said Mary's older relative, Elizabeth, was six months pregnant even though Elizabeth had been barren and was past normal child-bearing age. John's father was a Levitical priest who served twice a year in the Temple and raised John to be a devout Jew. Jesus and John were born into tumultuous times rife with religious groups and movements seeking prophetic voices and messianic hope.

As an adult, John the Baptist lived an austere life in the wilderness, wore camel's hair clothing, and ate locusts and wild honey. He preached a fiery message against religious corruption and social injustice, drawing large crowds of Jewish pilgrims from Jerusalem and beyond. His proclamation that the kingdom of heaven was near resonated deeply with people longing for deliverance from Roman rule. Many Jews saw John as a prophetic figure in the tradition of Elijah, fulfilling Malachi's prophecy of a forerunner who would prepare the way for the Messiah (Malachi 3:1).

Saint John the Baptist, Juan Martínez Montañés, ca. 1620–1630. Polychromed wood sculpture with gilding. Metropolitan Museum of Art, New York, New York, USA.

It was within this dramatic time in history that Jesus approached John for baptism.

Baptism was not a new practice in Jewish tradition. Ritual purification through immersion in water, known as the *mikveh*, was already common. However, John's baptism was distinct, because it emphasized repentance and preparation for the coming kingdom of God.

When John the Baptist initially resisted, recognizing Jesus's superiority, Jesus insisted, saying, "Let it be so now; it is proper for us to do this to fulfill all righteousness" (Matthew 3:15, NIV), indicating that his baptism was necessary to identify with humanity and fulfill God's plan. As Jesus emerged from the water, the heavens opened, and the Spirit of God descended like a dove, while a voice from heaven declared, "This is my beloved Son, in whom I am well pleased" (Matthew 3:17, KJV). This miraculous event confirmed Jesus's divine identity and mission.

The imagery of the dove had deep theological significance because doves were associated with purity, peace, and the presence of God. Doves were used in Temple sacrifices and became a symbol of the Holy Spirit in later Christian thought. The voice from heaven echoed Psalm 2:7 and Isaiah 42:1, reinforcing Jesus's role as the Son of God and the Suffering Servant.

The Baptism of Christ, Grigory Gagarin, ca. 1840–1850. Russian State Library, Moscow, Russia.

The Jordan River was also symbolically significant in Jewish history. It was the river that the Israelites, under Joshua's leadership, crossed to enter the Promised Land. By choosing this location for his baptism,

Jesus reenacted Israel's spiritual journey. But instead of entering a physical land, he initiated a new covenant with God's people.

Jesus's baptism also marked a transition from John the Baptist's ministry to Jesus's own. The event foreshadowed Christian baptism, which would later become a sacrament symbolizing repentance, spiritual rebirth, and initiation into the faith.

AND A VOICE
FROM HEAVEN SAID,
"THIS IS MY SON,
WHOM I LOVE;
WITH HIM I AM WELL PLEASED."

MATTHEW 3:17, NIV

THE BEGINNING OF JESUS'S MINISTRY

Christ in the Wilderness, Ivan Kramskoi, 1872.
State Tretyakov Gallery, Moscow, Russia.

Temptation in the Wilderness

Matthew 4:1–11

THEN WAS JESUS
LED UP OF THE SPIRIT
INTO THE
WILDERNESS
TO BE TEMPTED OF THE DEVIL.

MATTHEW 4:1, KJV

The dramatic moment of divine blessing at Jesus's baptism set the stage for a series of trials he had to face before officially beginning his teaching ministry. The narrative implies that Jesus was in some way compelled into the wilderness and spent almost six weeks there forgoing nourishment, presumably of any kind.

All the elements of this account were highly symbolic. Fasting was a practice seen throughout Jewish history, including Moses's fasting on Mount Sinai (see Exodus 34:28) and Elijah's journey to Mount Horeb (see 1 Kings 19:8). It was generally associated with supplication and contrition. Interestingly, throughout the Bible the number 40 often signified periods of trial and transformation.

The Spirit then Driveth Jesus into the Wilderness, William Hole, ca. 1906. Library of Congress Prints and Photographs Division, Washington, DC, USA.

The wilderness, which stretched east of Jerusalem to the Dead Sea, was known as *Yeshimmon*, meaning "devastation" in Hebrew. It is a barren, rocky region with little vegetation and extreme temperatures. Historically this kind of environment often symbolized personal testing and spiritual preparation. Today this area is predominately located in what is known as the West Bank. Although there are some water sources, average rainfall in this desert region is a meager three to four inches per year.

After nearly six weeks of harsh physical depravation, Jesus faced his most important tests. The narrative states that the devil, named by Jesus as Satan, appeared and presented three temptations that each held spiritual and cultural significance.

In a physically weakened state, hunger would have been an enormous test. Satan's challenge to turn stones into bread mirrored the Israelites' reliance on manna in the wilderness (see Exodus 16:4). Jesus responded with: "Man does not live on bread alone but on every word that comes from the mouth of the Lord" (Deuteronomy 8:3, NIV).

Then Satan transported Jesus to a high point in Jerusalem's Temple, possibly the southeastern corner, which had a 400-foot drop. The devil quoted Psalm 91:11–12, twisting scripture to challenge Jesus's trust in God's protection. Jesus rebuked him, saying: "Ye shall not tempt the Lord your God" (Deuteronomy 6:16, KJV).

The Temptation of Christ, Ary Scheffer, 1854. Walker Art Gallery, Liverpool, England, UK.

The final test took place on a high mountain, possibly symbolizing spiritual authority. Satan promised Jesus worldly power in exchange for worship, which Jesus rejected, demanding: "Away from me, Satan! For it is written: 'Worship the Lord your God, and serve him only'" (Matthew 4:10, NIV). This final refusal reaffirmed Jesus's mission as one of humility and obedience rather than earthly power.

After resisting these temptations, Satan departed, and angels came to minister to Jesus, signifying his victory over spiritual opposition. The Gospel of Mark adds an interesting detail that Jesus was "with the wild beasts" (Mark 1:13, KJV), which may have resonated with early Christian audiences in Rome, who were often persecuted and thrown to wild animals in arenas. His wilderness experience paralleled Israel's own 40-year journey. But where the Israelites often failed their tests, Jesus remained faithful, setting the tone for his ministry of righteousness and redemption. His trials were not just about personal testing but symbolized spiritual endurance amid worldly opposition.

WORSHIP THE LORD
YOUR GOD,
AND SERVE HIM ONLY.

MATTHEW 4:10, NIV

Calling the First Disciples

Mark 1:16–20

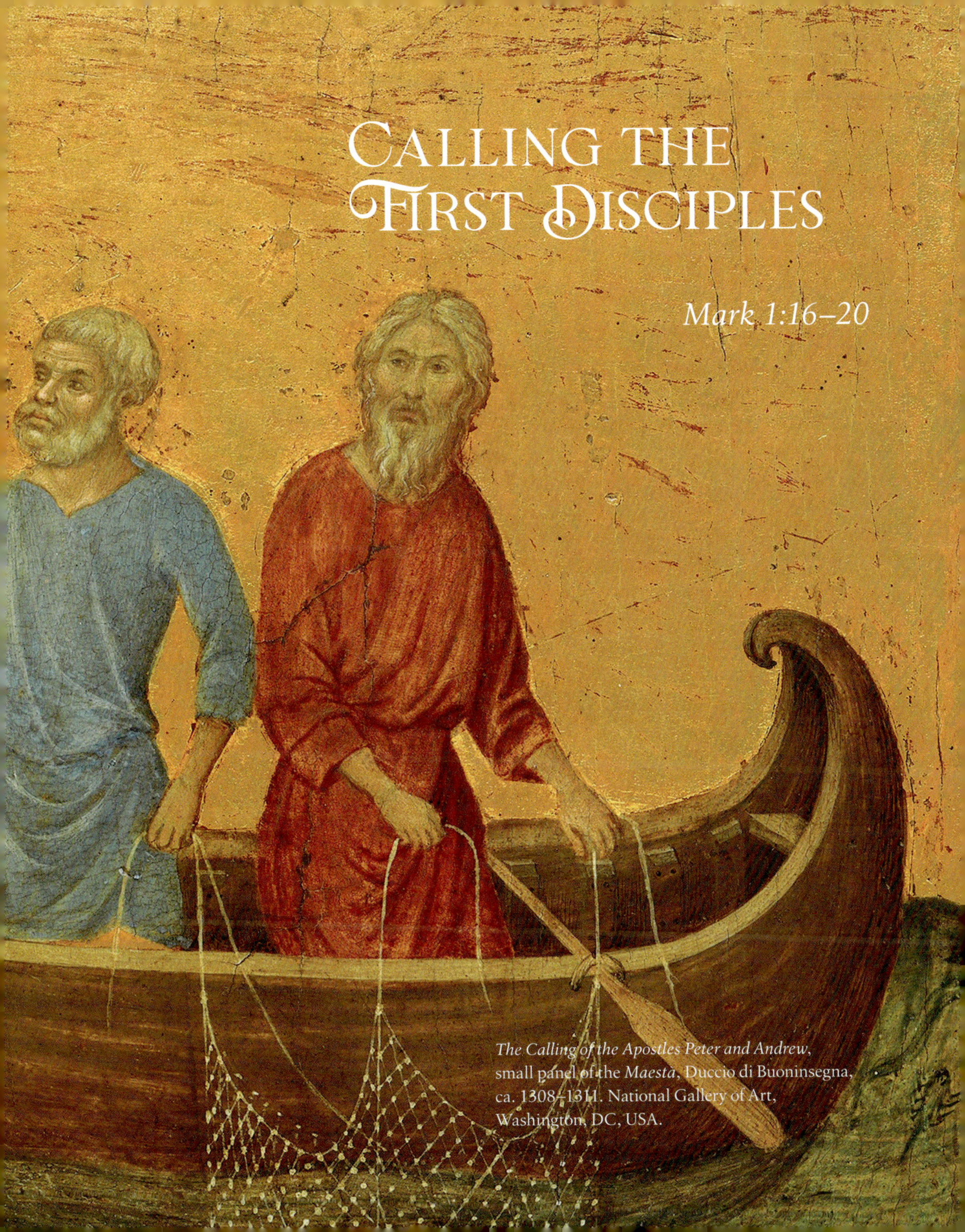

The Calling of the Apostles Peter and Andrew, small panel of the *Maestà*, Duccio di Buoninsegna, ca. 1308–1311. National Gallery of Art, Washington, DC, USA.

FOLLOW ME,
AND I WILL
MAKE YOU BECOME
FISHERS OF MEN.

MARK 1:17, ESV

After his wilderness experience, Jesus began his ministry in Capernaum and the surrounding area. Capernaum, located on the northwest edge of the Sea of Galilee near a fertile plain called Gennesaret, was home to approximately 1,500 residents in Jesus's lifetime.

The Sea of Galilee was a major center for fishing, and the fishermen often formed partnerships to maximize their catch. One such partnership—James, John, Simon Peter, and Andrew—were from Bethsaida, a community across the Jordan River on the northern side of the Sea of Galilee, roughly four miles from Capernaum. Both communities were heavily dependent on the region's main fish, a type of tilapia, which were salted and dried for exporting throughout the Roman Empire. This indigenous fish, sometimes called Saint Peter's fish, is still enjoyed in many homes and restaurants today.

The Calling of Andrew and Simon Peter, possibly a left wing of an altarpiece, follower of Rogier van der Weyden, ca. 1440. Upton House, Warwickshire, England, UK.

One day along the shore, Jesus encountered two pairs of brothers fishing—first Simon Peter and Andrew followed by James and John—and issued the men a surprising invitation to follow him and he would make them fish for people. This unusual invitation was both metaphorical and practical.

Fishing was hard, patient work, requiring not only skill but perseverance—qualities that would later help the disciples as they spread the gospel. Jesus's call implied that, just as they had cast their nets for fish, they would now cast a spiritual net to bring people into God's kingdom.

Another surprising aspect was that Jesus initiated the invitation himself. Although rabbis commonly had disciples, normally a disciple sought out the rabbi, not the other way around. The immediacy of the men's responses suggests either a deep trust in Jesus or a prior familiarity with his teachings as the economic and social impact of each man's decision to follow Jesus was significant. Fishing families were not necessarily poor—James and John's father,

The Calling of Saint Matthew, copy after Jan Sanders van Hemessen, early 1600s. Metropolitan Museum of Art, New York, New York, USA.

Zebedee, owned boats and employed hired men, suggesting he had a profitable business that his sons stood to inherit. Walking away from their livelihood meant abandoning financial security to follow Jesus into an uncertain future.

Jesus went on to gather twelve core disciples, among whom were people of diverse and sometimes conflicting backgrounds. Matthew, also called Levi, was a tax collector and viewed as a traitor for working with the Romans, whereas Simon the Zealot was likely affiliated with sometimes violent anti-Roman resistance movements. Beyond the Twelve, as they are sometimes known, there were many other people who supported Jesus including key women such as James and John's mother, Salome (cf. Matthew 27:56; Mark 15:40–41); Mary Magdelene, from whom seven demons had gone out; and Joanna, the wife of Herod Antipas's steward (Luke 8:2–3). Bringing together people from such various backgrounds under a unified mission was a radical act of reconciliation and transformation.

Jesus's call marked the beginning of a new kind of discipleship, one that went beyond studying scripture to active participation. The disciples' journey would be one of learning, sacrifice, and transformation, as they transitioned from fishermen to leaders of the early Christian movement.

AT ONCE

THEY LEFT THEIR NETS

AND

FOLLOWED HIM.

MARK 1:18, NIV

WEDDING AT CANA

John 2:1–11

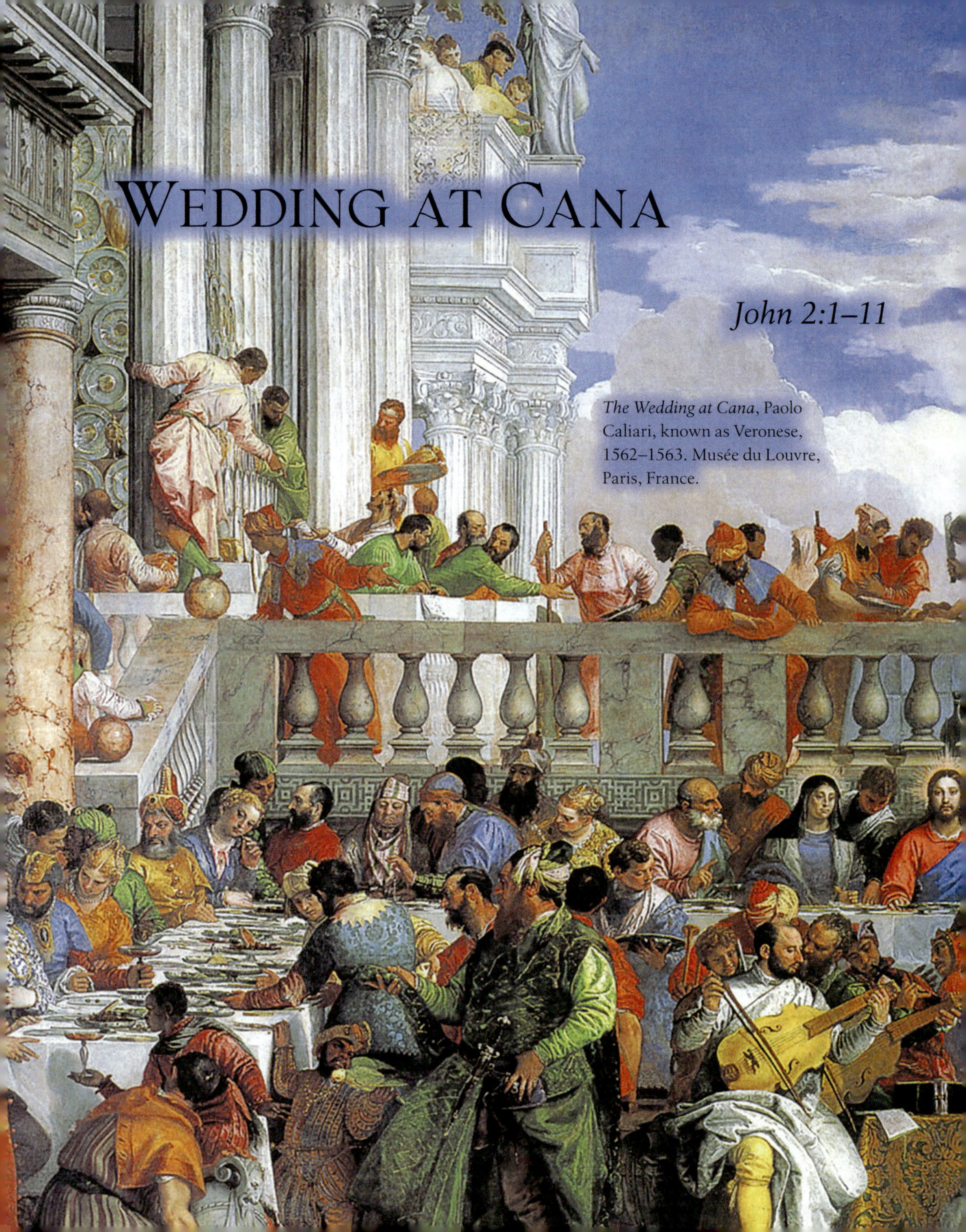

The Wedding at Cana, Paolo Caliari, known as Veronese, 1562–1563. Musée du Louvre, Paris, France.

WHAT JESUS DID HERE
IN CANA OF GALILEE
WAS THE FIRST OF THE SIGNS
THROUGH WHICH HE REVEALED
HIS GLORY;
AND HIS DISCIPLES
BELIEVED IN HIM.

JOHN 2:11, NIV

To the casual observer, Jesus initially appeared to be simply a devout rabbi, a skilled and engaging teacher who had a small band of followers. It was in those early days that Jesus and his disciples were invited to a wedding in Cana, likely a town near Nazareth.

Weddings in first-century Jewish culture were major social events and often lasted up to seven days. The entire community participated, and it was the responsibility of the groom and his family to host their guests with food, drink, and anything else guests needed throughout the entire celebration. Weddings were a significant undertaking for the host family and running out of anything would have been a humiliating failure in hospitality, a key virtue in Jewish society.

It was that precise scenario that was noticed by Mary, Jesus's mother, and she promptly informed Jesus that the wine had run out. Her actions are significant because they both

Marriage at Cana, fresco by unknown artist, ca. 1350. Visoki Dečani Monastery, Deçan, Kosovo.

demonstrate her concern for the host family and seem to imply belief that Jesus could do something to solve the problem. Jesus's response, "Woman, why do you involve me?" (John 2:4, NIV) sounds shocking in English, but the Greek word used for "woman" was a formal expression rather than a disrespectful rebuff. He went on to claim that his divine mission was not yet fully revealed.

But Jesus still chose to act. He instructed the servants to fill six stone jars with water. These containers, holding 20–30 gallons each, were used for ritual purification under Jewish law. Wine held deep symbolic meaning in Jewish tradition. It was a sign of joy and divine blessing and often associated with the coming messianic age (Isaiah 25:6). By transforming this water into wine, Jesus subtly redefined traditional purification rites, signaling a new spiritual era.

The transformation from water to wine was instantaneous and of the highest quality, as noted by the master of the feast, who was unaware of the miracle. It was so good, in fact, that the master of the feast praised the bridegroom for going above and beyond by serving quality wine well into the celebration, a point at which most people started serving wine of a lesser quality. The abundance of superior wine in this miracle hinted of Jesus's role in bringing spiritual renewal.

Marriage at Cana (detail), fresco in *Cycle of the Life of the Christ*, middle tier north wall, Giotto, 1304–1306. Scrovegni Chapel, Padua, Veneto, Italy.

This event also highlighted Jesus's compassion and willingness to engage in everyday human experiences. Unlike later miracles of healing or exorcism, this act was quiet and behind the scenes, benefiting the wedding guests without drawing immediate attention. The disciples witnessed this miracle, deepening their faith and marking the beginning of Jesus's public ministry. The significance of Jesus's first recorded miracle being that of turning water into wine remains a powerful symbol of transformation, celebration, and the arrival of God's kingdom.

THE MASTER OF THE BANQUET TASTED THE WATER THAT HAD BEEN TURNED INTO WINE . . . THEN HE CALLED THE BRIDEGROOM ASIDE AND SAID, ". . . YOU HAVE SAVED THE BEST TILL NOW."

JOHN 2:9–10, NIV

Indiction, fresco by unknown artist, ca. 1350. Visoki Dečani Monastery, Deçan, Kosovo.

Jesus Proclaims His Purpose

Luke 4:14–21

XC

THE SPIRIT OF THE LORD
IS ON ME,
BECAUSE HE HAS
ANOINTED ME
TO PROCLAIM
GOOD NEWS
TO THE POOR.

LUKE 4:18a, NIV

While Jesus was circumspect when he performed his first miracle, his next recorded action was anything but subtle and sparked a controversy that followed him for the rest of his ministry.

Nazareth at the time was a small village of only a few hundred people, located near major trade routes yet still relatively insignificant compared to larger cities such as Sepphoris and Tiberias. The inhabitants were devoutly Jewish, maintaining strong messianic expectations due to the oppressive Roman occupation of Judea and Galilee. Many Jews, including the close-knit community living in Nazareth, longed for a political deliverer known as Messiah, who would restore the glory of Israel.

It was in this religiously charged environment before his family, friends, and neighbors that Jesus made the deeply significant choice to read from Isaiah 61 in the synagogue in Nazareth. Synagogues played a central role in Jewish religious and community life particularly in smaller towns and villages, where they served as places of prayer, study, and legal proceedings. The practice of reading from the Torah and the Prophets on the sabbath was an integral part of synagogue worship, with passages often chosen according to an established cycle. It would have been common to choose a local rabbi to read from the scroll when he was visiting his hometown.

A scroll of the book of Isaiah. Photo credit: Pete Unseth, 2009.

The passage Jesus read (Isaiah 61:1–2a) describes the Messiah as one anointed by God to bring good news, heal the brokenhearted, and proclaim liberty. However, Jesus stopped reading just before the portion about God's vengeance for which the Jewish people longed (see Isaiah 61:2b), which suggested he followed a spiritual rather than political mission. His declaration, "Today this scripture is fulfilled in your hearing," shocked the congregation, because through that statement he explicitly claimed to be the fulfillment of the ancient prophecy.

Initially, everyone in the synagogue marveled at Jesus's words and seemed surprised because they knew him as the local carpenter's son not an eloquent and inspired rabbi. Yet Jesus seemed to know that his words would not be well received by his hometown when he said, "No prophet is accepted in his hometown."

The Brow of the Hill Near Nazareth, James Tissot, ca. 1886–1894. Brooklyn Museum, Brooklyn, New York, USA.

The people's amazement quickly turned to anger when Jesus went on to reference stories of Elijah and Elisha, pointing out where God's miracles benefited Gentiles rather than Israelites. His statements implied that God's salvation was for all people, not just Jews, contradicting the nationalistic hopes of his audience. Enraged, the people Jesus grew up with—friends and neighbors—drove him out of town intending to throw him off a cliff, which was a common method of execution for blasphemy at that time.

This stunning incident foreshadowed the widespread rejection Jesus would face, especially from the religious authorities. It also highlighted his radical message of inclusion and spiritual deliverance, rather than the expected political revolution against Rome.

HE HAS SENT ME
TO PROCLAIM FREEDOM
FOR THE PRISONERS
AND RECOVERY OF SIGHT
FOR THE BLIND,
TO SET THE OPPRESSED FREE,
TO PROCLAIM THE YEAR OF
THE LORD'S FAVOR.

LUKE 4:18b–19, NIV

The Beatitudes

Matthew 5:1–12

Sermon on the Mountain, Károly Ferenczy, 1896. Magyar Nemzeti Galéria, Budapest, Hungary.

BLESSED ARE
THE POOR IN SPIRIT:
FOR THEIRS IS
THE KINGDOM OF HEAVEN.
BLESSED ARE
THEY THAT MOURN:
FOR THEY SHALL
BE COMFORTED.
BLESSED ARE THE MEEK:
FOR THEY SHALL
INHERIT THE EARTH.

MATTHEW 5:3–5, KJV

In the first months of Jesus's ministry, he traveled the area near Capernaum preaching and teaching. As word spread, people from as far away as Jerusalem—at least a week's journey by foot—traveled to wherever he was at the time to hear him speak. Sometimes that was a follower's house in town. Sometimes it was on the Sea of Galilee shoreline. One day such a crowd gathered, and Jesus climbed part way up a mountain overlooking the Sea so the people could see and hear him. The teaching he gave that day became known in history as the Sermon on the Mount.

Jesus began with a series of profound statements about what kinds of people are blessed and their subsequent rewards. These statements, now called Beatitudes from the Latin word *beatitudo*, meaning "happiness" or "blessedness," outlined a radical reversal of worldly values and prioritized people who were humble, merciful, or persecuted over powerful and privileged people. There are two versions of the Beatitudes recorded. The version in Luke includes similar blessings but adds corresponding woes, reinforcing a social critique (Luke 6:20–26, KJV). Some scholars believe Matthew emphasized spiritual blessings, while Luke highlighted tangible, earthly realities.

Interestingly the physically elevated position Jesus took that day to teach would have reinforced associations his Jewish listeners had with divine revelations

"The Eight Beatitudes," folio from Walters manuscript W.171, Dirc van Delf, ca. 1400–1404. Walters Art Museum, Baltimore, MD, USA.

such as when Moses received the Law on Mount Sinai. But where Moses conveyed legal commandments, Jesus challenged conventional expectations and focused on inward transformation, reflecting a new understanding of righteousness:

- **Blessed are the poor in spirit:** Jesus emphasized spiritual humility and dependence on God contrary to traditional Jewish thought that linked material blessings to divine favor.
- **Blessed are they that mourn:** Jesus affirmed grief as a path to divine comfort in a society that viewed suffering as a sign of divine punishment.
- **Blessed are the meek:** Roman and Jewish societies often valued power and strength, yet Jesus promised that the gentle would inherit the earth.
- **Blessed are they which do hunger and thirst after righteousness:** Jesus called for a deep longing for justice and holiness in place of personal ambition or political power.
- **Blessed are the merciful:** Jesus advocated compassion and forgiveness while Roman law emphasized retribution.

Jesus Preaching on the Mountain, Gustave Doré, 1865–1868. Location unknown.

- **Blessed are the pure in heart:** Jesus highlighted internal sincerity while Jewish purity laws focused on external rituals.
- **Blessed are the peacemakers:** Jesus upheld peace as a divine virtue in an era of political rebellion against Rome.
- **Blessed are they which are persecuted:** Jesus offered heavenly vindication for righteous people instead of earthly rewards.

These statements echoed themes from Jewish texts, particularly Isaiah 61:1–2 where the prophet spoke of bringing good news to the poor and brokenhearted. This further connected Jesus's teaching to Jewish messianic expectations, yet his message subverted traditional assumptions about power and divine favor. The Beatitudes invited listeners to embody the values of God's kingdom rather than worldly aspirations, and they set the foundation for Jesus's broader teachings on love, justice, and discipleship. These same radical values continue to shape Christian ethics today, emphasizing humility, mercy, and spiritual longing over material wealth and social status.

BLESSED ARE
THE PURE IN HEART:
FOR THEY SHALL SEE GOD.
BLESSED ARE THE PEACEMAKERS:
FOR THEY SHALL BE CALLED
THE CHILDREN OF GOD.

MATTHEW 5:8–9, KJV

The Lord's Prayer

Matthew 6:7–13

Sermon on the Mount, Fritz von Uhde, ca. 1877. Museum of Fine Arts, Budapest, Hungary.

OUR FATHER
WHICH ART IN HEAVEN,
HALLOWED BE THY NAME.
THY KINGDOM COME,
THY WILL BE DONE IN EARTH,
AS IT IS IN HEAVEN.

MATTHEW 6:9–10, KJV

Some of Jesus's most famous words are recorded in Matthew 6. These few short sentences, known today as the Lord's Prayer or the Our Father, form one of the most widely recited prayers in Christianity. Like the Beatitudes, this beloved prayer is part of Jesus's Sermon on the Mount in which he taught on various aspects of civil and religious life.

Jesus modeled simplicity and directness when addressing God in direct contrast to the long, elaborate prayers of religious leaders of that time. His opening words, "Our Father," were revolutionary. God was often seen as a distant and sovereign ruler in Jewish tradition, yet Jesus invited listeners to approach God as a loving Father. This reflected the *Abba* concept (Aramaic for "Father"), which emphasized both authority and tenderness. But Jesus contrasted that by declaring God's name to be holy. Jews consider the divine name (YHWH) too sacred to speak aloud. Jesus's declaration, "Hallowed be thy name," reflected this reverence and reminded listeners to live in a way that sanctified God's name.

But when ye pray use not vain repetitions. as the heathen do for they think that they shall be heard for their much speaking.

Be not ye therefore like unto them : for your Father knoweth what things ye have need of, before ye ask him.

After this manner therefore pray ye :

Our Father which art in heaven, Hallowed be thy name. Thy kingdom come. Thy will be done in earth, as it is in heaven. Give

"The Lord's Prayer," from *The Sermon on the Mount*, Folio 17-18, Owen Carter Jones, published by Longman & Co., 1845.

Jesus then expressed a deep longing for God's rule to be fully realized on earth. Many first-century Jews awaited a military Messiah who would establish a political kingdom free from Roman rule. Today Jewish people hold various beliefs about Messiah, from a metaphor for a better future to a literal human descendant of King David who establishes worldwide justice and peace. Interestingly, Jesus's teaching on prayer pointed to a *spiritual* kingdom characterized by righteousness, peace, and submission to God's will.

His prayer also included a request for daily bread, symbolizing total dependence on God for all necessities. This echoed God's provision of manna to the Israelites (Exodus 16) and reinforced the concept that God daily sustains his people.

Jesus then highlighted the reciprocal nature of forgiveness and mercy. In Jewish law at the time, debts were often financial, but Jesus expanded the concept to include moral and spiritual obligations (see Matthew 6:14–15). His assertion that God's forgiveness was contingent upon a person's willingness to forgive others was a radical teaching in a culture where justice often meant strict repayment and retribution.

us this day our daily bread, and
forgive us our debts as we for-
give our debtors. And lead us
not into temptation, but deliver
us from evil: For thine is the
kingdom, and the power, and
the glory, for ever: Amen.

For if ye forgive men their
trespasses, your heavenly
Father will also forgive you.

But if ye forgive not men
their trespasses, neither
will your Father forgive
your trespasses.

Moreover, when ye fast, be
not as the hypocrites, of a
sad countenance: for they
disfigure their faces, that they

"The Lord's Prayer," from *The Sermon on the Mount*, Folio 17-18, Owen Carter Jones, published by Longman & Co., 1845.

Next, Jesus acknowledged the spiritual struggles humans face. While God does not tempt anyone to sin (see James 1:13), his petition asked for protection from trials, moral failures, and the schemes of the evil one, a concept well-established in Jewish thought (see the book of Job; Matthew 4:1–11).

The conclusion of this famous prayer, often called the Doxology, affirmed that God alone reigns supreme and reinforced the theme of divine authority. Although the words "For thine is the kingdom, and the power, and the glory, forever" are consistent with the message and format of Jesus's prayer, they are not found in the earliest manuscript sources for the Gospel of Matthew. It is believed they were incorporated in the late first or early second century. But together with Jesus's words this became the model prayer for Christians for nearly 2,000 years, uniting them across various traditions in a shared expression of faith. This prayer remains radical in its simplicity, inclusivity, and emphasis on a relationship with God.

FOR THINE IS
THE KINGDOM,
AND THE POWER,
AND THE GLORY, FOR EVER.
AMEN.

MATTHEW 6:13b, KJV

Parables & Teachings of Jesus

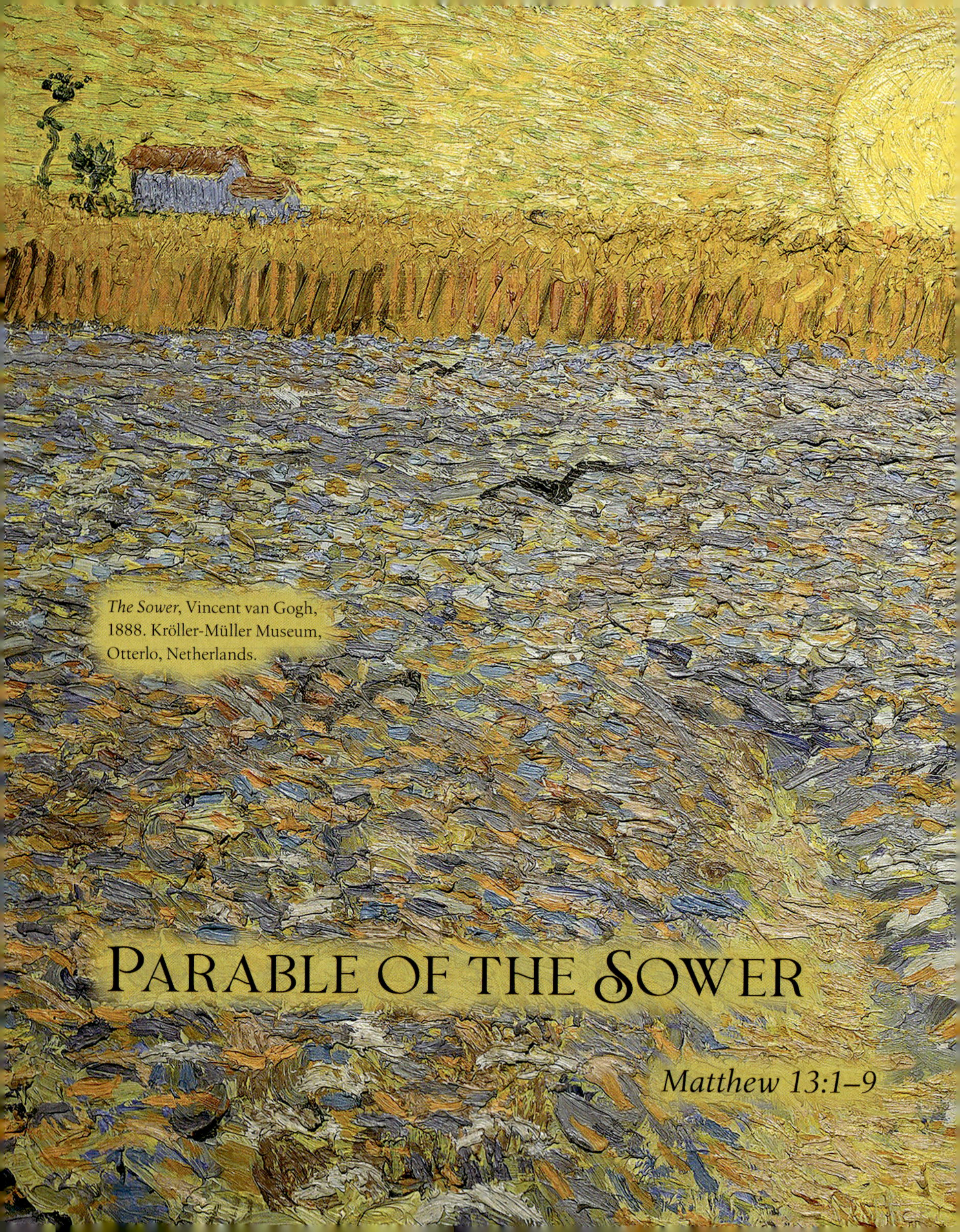

The Sower, Vincent van Gogh, 1888. Kröller-Müller Museum, Otterlo, Netherlands.

Parable of the Sower

Matthew 13:1–9

AS HE WAS
SCATTERING THE SEED,
SOME FELL ALONG THE PATH,
AND THE BIRDS CAME AND
ATE IT UP . . .
STILL OTHER SEED FELL ON
GOOD SOIL, WHERE IT
PRODUCED A CROP.

MATTHEW 13:4, 8, NIV

Jesus spent much of his three years in public ministry traveling to various locations around Capernaum, where he would often teach using parables, which are short stories or illustrations with vivid imagery familiar to the audience. As Jesus gained popularity, increasing numbers of people traveled to where he was to listen to him. So many people gathered the day Jesus told the parable of the sower, that he had to teach from a boat on the Sea of Galilee while the crowd listened from the shore. This method of teaching in open-air settings was common for itinerant Jewish teachers and allowed large audiences to hear without other means of amplification.

This setting was also significant because the region was rich in agricultural imagery. Farming was a common occupation in Jesus's lifetime, and sowing seeds was a practice familiar to his audience. Many of his listeners that day had likely experienced the very scenarios he described because their fields, while typically plowed, contained varying types of soil ranging from fertile ground to rocky paths. Jesus's use of common farming metaphors helped listeners relate to the deeper spiritual meaning he conveyed. But although the parables he told started on familiar ground, they were filled with plot twists and unexpected reversals and challenged listeners to think deeply about moral, social, and religious matters.

Parable of the Sower, Antonios Fikos, 2012. Used with permission.

For the parable of the sower, Jesus later explained to his disciples that the seeds represented the message of God's kingdom, while the different types of soil symbolized how people receive and respond to the message (Matthew 13:18–23):

- The path represented people who heard the message of God's kingdom but did not understand it, so its truth was quickly snatched away.
- The rocky ground symbolized people who initially received the message about God's kingdom with joy but abandoned their faith when trouble arose, because they lacked roots to support them.
- Growing among thorns described people whose faith in God's kingdom was overcome and choked out by worldly worries and materialism.
- Good soil represented people who heard, understood, and acted according to the message of God's kingdom, producing a rich spiritual harvest.

Christ of the Cornfield, Kuzma Petrov-Vodkin, 1914. Location unknown.

Jesus's teaching about spiritual growth and perseverance challenged the expectations of his audience, who deeply desired the arrival of *Mashiach* (Hebrew for Messiah), the foretold Jewish leader who would rid them of the hated Romans and usher in an age of peace and prosperity. They expected the Messiah to bring immediate political transformation and relief from oppression. The idea of the kingdom of God growing slowly like a crop contrasted with the popular apocalyptic hopes for an abrupt overthrow of Roman rule.

The parable of the sower was just one of many parables that Jesus used to illustrate the nature of God's kingdom, which grows gradually, unseen, and with varied results among individuals. By explaining the meaning of the parable to his disciples privately, Jesus reinforced the importance of deeper spiritual understanding over simply hearing the words. This lesson emphasized discipleship and commitment, crucial themes that defined Jesus's ministry.

THEN HE TOLD THEM
MANY THINGS IN PARABLES . . .
WHOEVER HAS EARS,
LET THEM HEAR.

MATTHEW 13:3, 9, NIV

Parable of the Good Samaritan

Luke 10:25–37

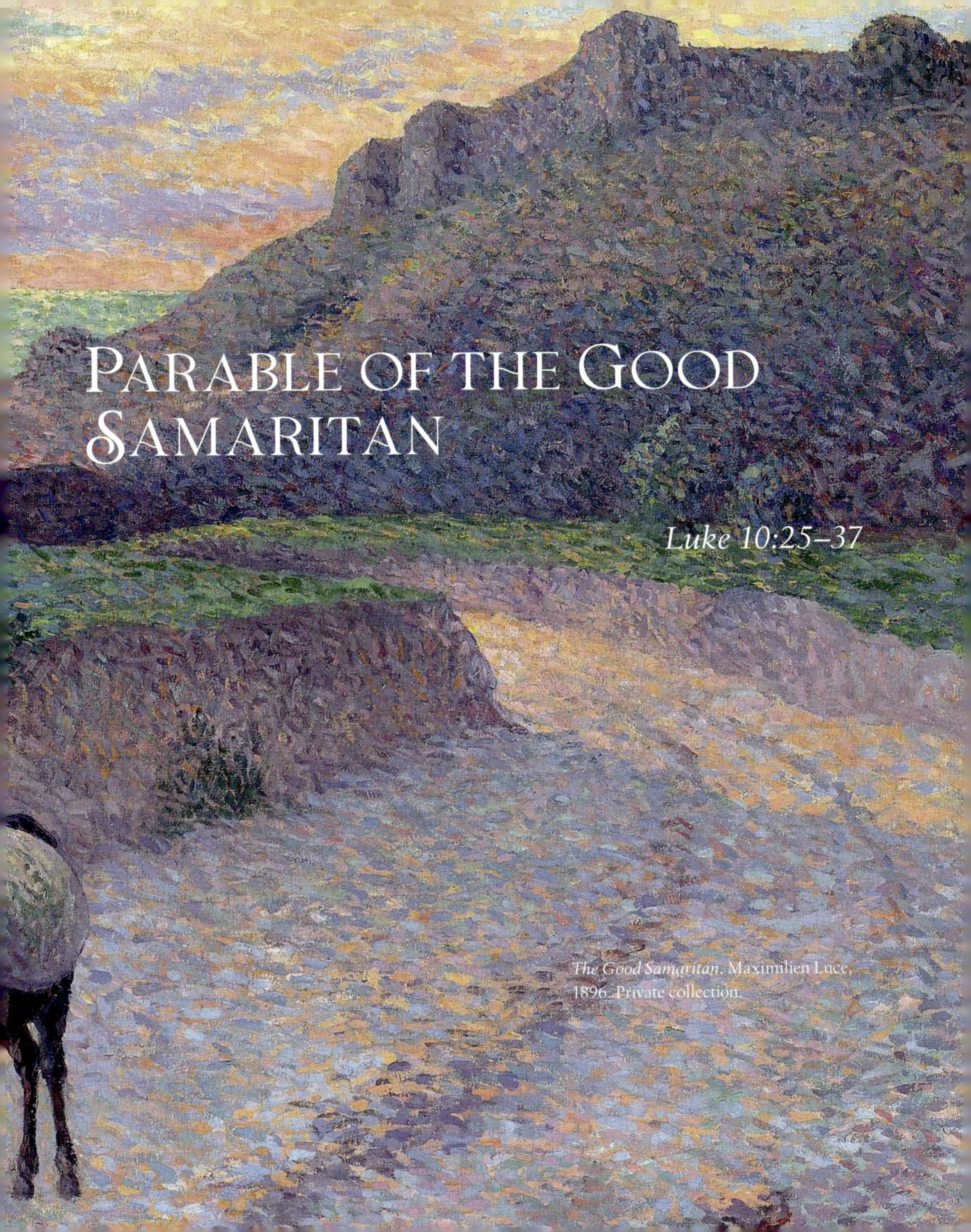

The Good Samaritan, Maximilien Luce, 1896. Private collection.

YOU SHALL LOVE THE LORD
YOUR GOD
WITH ALL YOUR HEART
AND WITH ALL
YOUR SOUL
AND WITH ALL YOUR STRENGTH
AND WITH ALL YOUR MIND,
AND YOUR NEIGHBOR
AS YOURSELF.

LUKE 10:27, ESV

Accounts of Jesus's life repeatedly demonstrate he was a person who produced strong reactions: people either loved him and his teachings or they despised him and looked for ways to silence him. Opponents often tried to trap him. Others tried to justify themselves when Jesus's teaching made them uncomfortable.

In one such instance, an expert in the religious law and the Hebrew Bible attempted to assess Jesus's ability to interpret Mosaic law by asking how to inherit eternal life. Jesus astutely turned the question back on the lawyer, who responded correctly to love God and to love one's neighbor (Deuteronomy 6:5; Leviticus 19:18). But his next question, "Who is my neighbor?" brought a stunning response in the form of the parable of the Good Samaritan, one of Jesus's most well-known teachings. The prevailing Jewish understanding was that a neighbor meant a fellow Israelite, but Jesus's story redefined the term, making it clear that a true neighbor is anyone in need, regardless of that person's background.

The Good Samaritan, George Frederic Watts, 1850. Manchester Art Gallery, Manchester, England, UK.

The setting of the story—the road from Jerusalem to Jericho—was a notoriously dangerous route known as the Bloody Pass. The 17-mile stretch of road descended more than 3,000 feet in elevation, winding through rocky terrain and providing ample opportunities for ambush by robbers.

In Jesus's time, priests and Levites were esteemed religious figures responsible for maintaining Temple worship. They could have ignored the wounded man, thinking he was dead, because ritual purity laws prohibited their contact with a corpse (Numbers 19:11–13). Some scholars have theorized that they could also have been concerned that the robbers were still near, and they would be the next victims. Both reasons seem plausible, but in Jesus's parable, their lack of compassion contrasted starkly with the actions of the Samaritan.

Samaritans were deeply despised by Jewish people due to centuries of hostility. This animosity originated from historical conflicts, differing religious practices, and intermarriage. The two *denarii* that the Samaritan man gave the innkeeper were equivalent to two days' wages and a significant sum to cover the wounded man's care. This act highlighted the extent of his generosity and the self-sacrificial nature of true mercy. By making a Samaritan the hero of the story, Jesus challenged the deep-seated prejudices of his time and emphasized that true neighborly love transcends racial and social divisions.

The Parable of the Good Samaritan, Edward Carter Preston, 1921. Memorial window to the parents of Selwyn Lloyd, MP, Speaker of the House of Commons, north aisle of West Kirby Methodist Church, West Kirby, Merseyside, England, UK.

The profound lesson of the Good Samaritan remains highly relevant today and continues to inspire hospitals, charities, and legal principles worldwide. Even well-known figures including Dr. Martin Luther King Jr. have referenced this parable, emphasizing the moral obligation to show compassion to people beyond social and ethnic boundaries, even at great personal risk. This is made even more impactful by the fact that Dr. King made this reference the night before his assassination. Ultimately, the parable of the Good Samaritan continues to call people to embody radical love and compassion in their daily lives.

"WHICH OF THESE THREE,
DO YOU THINK,
PROVED TO BE A NEIGHBOR
TO THE MAN WHO FELL AMONG
THE ROBBERS?" HE SAID,
"THE ONE WHO SHOWED HIM
MERCY."
AND JESUS SAID TO HIM,
"YOU GO, AND DO LIKEWISE."

LUKE 10:36–37, ESV

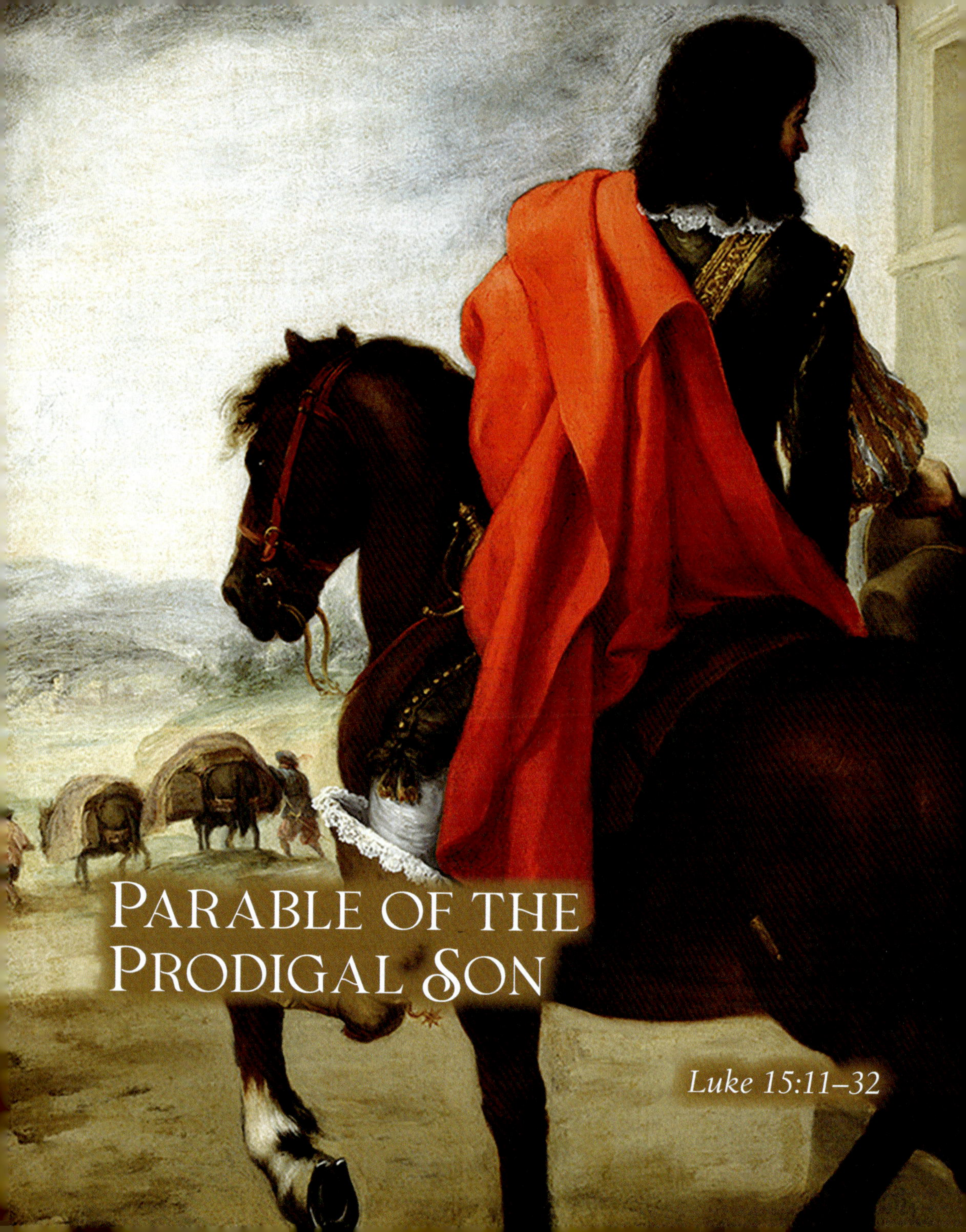

Parable of the Prodigal Son

Luke 15:11–32

The Departure of the Prodigal Son, Bartolomé Esteban Murillo, 1660s. National Gallery of Ireland, Dublin, Ireland.

AND HE AROSE
AND CAME TO HIS FATHER.
BUT WHILE HE WAS STILL
A LONG WAY OFF,
HIS FATHER SAW HIM
AND FELT COMPASSION, AND RAN
AND EMBRACED HIM
AND KISSED HIM.

LUKE 15:20, ESV

The parable of the prodigal son is one of Jesus's most well-known parables, rich in cultural, religious, and social meaning. It is one of three parables recorded in Luke 15, along with the lost sheep and lost coin, all illustrating themes of redemption, mercy, and forgiveness, which Jesus told in response to religious leaders grumbling there were "tax collectors and sinners" (Luke 15:1–2) gathered to hear Jesus teach.

In the parable, a father's younger son demanded his inheritance early, a deeply offensive action in Jewish society. Under Jewish inheritance laws, the eldest son received a double portion, while the younger received one-third of the estate (Deuteronomy 21:17). However, asking for an inheritance before the father's death was equivalent to wishing him dead.

Surprisingly, the father granted the younger son's wish, and the young man quickly left for a far country, where he squandered his wealth in wild living.

The Prodigal Son, Jacob Jordaens, 1640. Gemäldegalerie Alte Meister, Dresden, Germany.

His actions reflected a theme of reckless independence that starkly contrasted with Jewish values of family honor and responsibility. When famine struck, the man was forced to tend pigs, an occupation that was the most degrading imaginable for a Jew and unclean under Jewish law (Leviticus 11:7). Shockingly, the once free and privileged son of a Jewish landowner was now a swineherd in a foreign land.

When he realized his mistake, the young man decided to return home and beg for forgiveness, expecting to be treated as a hired servant. According to tradition, a father suffering such dishonorable treatment must either reject or severely punish his son. However, this father's reaction was radical: he *ran* to meet and embrace his lost son, a completely undignified act for a patriarch in Middle Eastern culture. Overjoyed, the father called for the best robe, a ring, and sandals—all symbols of restored sonship and authority.

But Jesus didn't end the parable at the happy ending. He went on to detail the elder brother's less-than-favorable response, whose resentment reflected a legalistic righteousness, a viewpoint that mirrored the Pharisees' attitudes toward Jesus's welcoming sinners. But the father showed his oldest son equal graciousness, addressing him as "my son" and validating his rightful place, declaring, "All this is yours and you are with me always." This final scene with the elder brother illustrates that Jesus was not simply telling a heartwarming story about the return of a wayward son. Nor was it a fairy tale where everyone lived "happily ever after." Rather, it left questions unanswered and invited personal reflection.

The Return of the Prodigal Son, Father, Andrei Mironov, 2023. Ryazan, Russia. Used with permission.

Interestingly, the word *prodigal* means "recklessly extravagant." Although the word is typically applied to the younger son, the father also provided recklessly extravagant demonstrations of love to both of his sons. The father ran to greet the son who had lost his way when he openly rejected his father. Similarly, the father sought out the oldest who lived amid rich blessings and yet was lost in his feelings of bitterness. With this parable, Jesus invited listeners to identify with both sons—the wayward sinner in need of forgiveness and the self-righteous individual struggling with grace.

LET US
EAT AND CELEBRATE.
FOR THIS MY SON WAS DEAD,
AND IS ALIVE AGAIN;
HE WAS LOST, AND IS FOUND.

LUKE 15:23b–24a, ESV

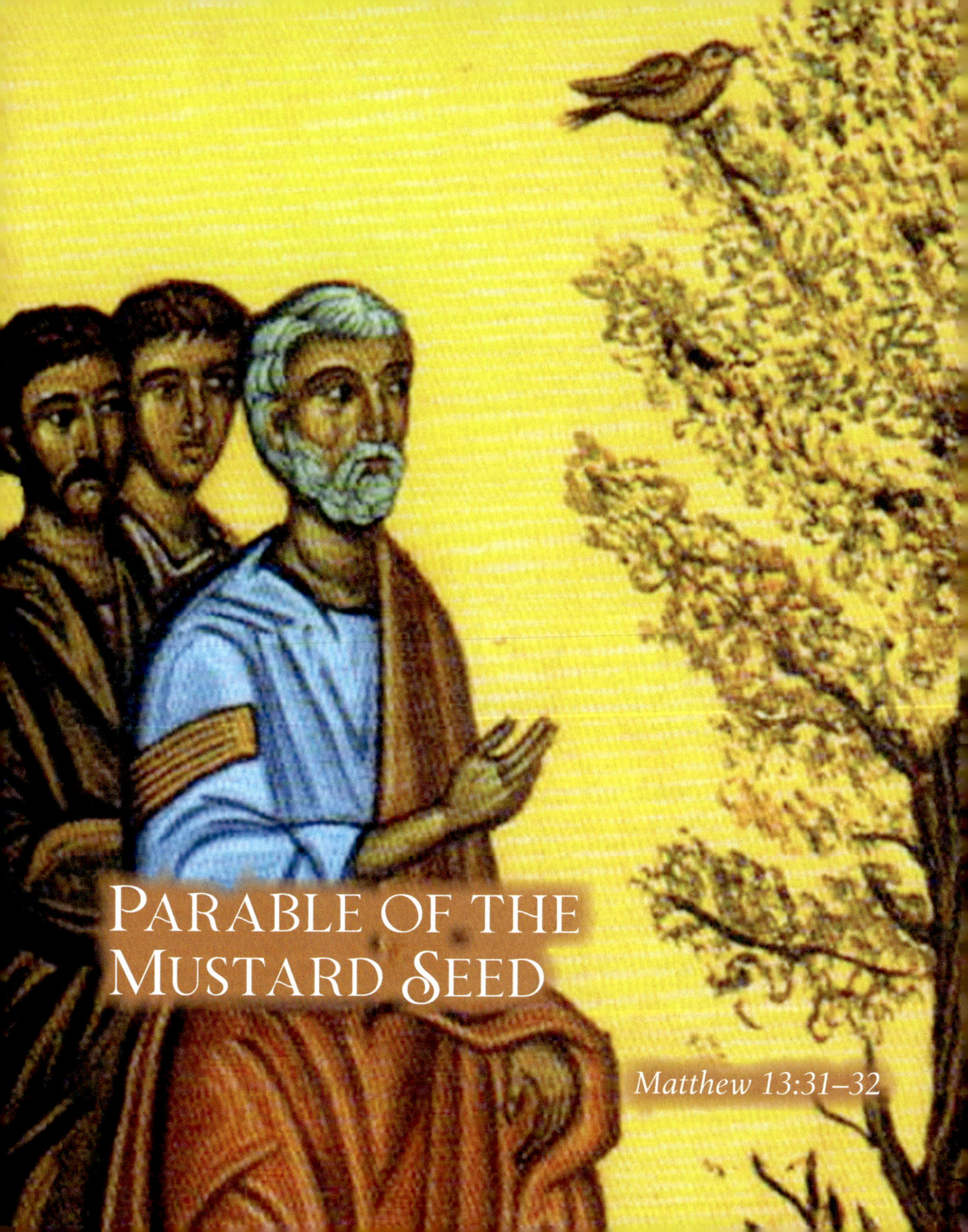

Parable of the Mustard Seed

Matthew 13:31–32

Jesus and the Parable of the Mustard Seed icon, unknown.

THE KINGDOM OF HEAVEN
IS LIKE A GRAIN
OF MUSTARD SEED . . .
WHEN IT HAS GROWN
IT IS LARGER THAN ALL
THE GARDEN PLANTS . . .
SO THAT THE BIRDS
OF THE AIR COME AND MAKE
NESTS IN ITS BRANCHES.

MATTHEW 13:31–32, ESV

Perhaps one of Jesus's most vivid illustrations of the kingdom of God is found in two short verses referred to as the parable of the mustard seed. This parable is recorded in three of the Gospels—Matthew, Mark, and Luke. In both Matthew and Luke, this parable is followed immediately by the parable of the leaven, which shares the theme of small beginnings.

Mustard plants are known for their rapid growth, and the entire plant, from roots to flowers, is edible. It is believed that the black mustard plant, *brassica nigra*, was grown in first-century Galilee. Several kinds of mustard, including black mustard, have been cultivated for centuries and used for food, in wine, as medicine, and even in the burial of Egyptian pharaohs. The mustard plant is still grown and its seeds harvested today, although the plant is considered invasive in many regions, pointing to its extreme hardiness and resilience.

The black mustard seed is tiny: approximately one to two millimeters in diameter, which is roughly the width of the line made by a medium ballpoint pen. While it was among the smallest seeds a first-century farmer might sow, it could grow into a bush as large as 10 feet tall. This would have been a striking image for Jesus's audience, emphasizing how something seemingly insignificant could expand beyond expectation.

Illustration of *brassica nigra* (black mustard), Walther Otto Müller, 1897.

The comparison of God's kingdom to a growing seed reflected themes found in Jewish wisdom literature and the Old Testament. Specifically, the imagery of a tree with birds nesting in its branches echoed Daniel 4:12 and Ezekiel 17:23, where large trees represented kingdoms that provided shelter and influence. Jesus's use of this metaphor suggested that God's rule would begin humbly but eventually encompass all nations.

Many of Jesus's listeners would have been farmers familiar with the agricultural cycle. Planting and harvesting were central to Jewish life and religious festivals, and parables about seeds and growth were particularly relatable. The idea that the smallest seed could produce a great tree challenged traditional expectations of a powerful messiah, reinforcing that God's kingdom would emerge gradually and unexpectedly.

Mustard trees, National Park Service photographer, 2025. Santa Monica Mountains National Recreation Area, California, USA.

Illustration of European goldfinch, unknown artist, *Birds and Nature Vol. XIII*, A. W. Mumford Publisher, 1903. Smithsonian Libraries, Washington, DC, USA.

In a Roman-occupied world where the Jewish people awaited a military or political deliverer, this parable suggested that God's kingdom would expand not by force but by transformation from within. Early Christians later interpreted this parable as a metaphor for the spread of the gospel, beginning with Jesus and his small group of disciples and growing into a global faith.

Jesus often used familiar elements from daily life to illustrate deep theological truths. The mustard plant, though common, symbolized unexpected greatness, much like his followers—ordinary people called to spread an extraordinary message. The birds nesting in its branches further underscored the idea that God's kingdom would welcome all nations.

This parable remains one of Jesus's most enduring teachings, emphasizing faith, perseverance, and the transformative power of God's kingdom.

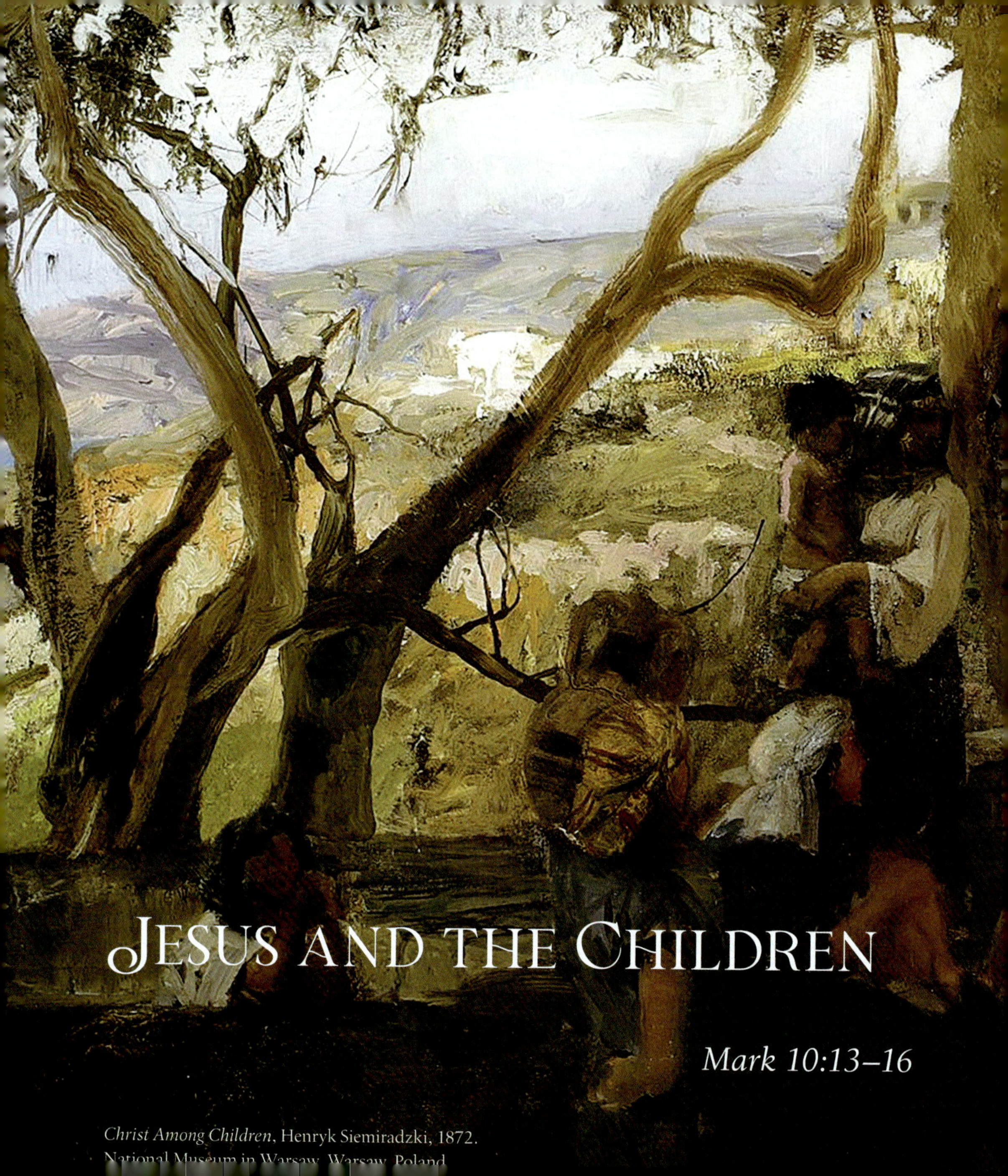

Jesus and the Children

Mark 10:13–16

Christ Among Children, Henryk Siemiradzki, 1872.
National Museum in Warsaw, Warsaw, Poland

SUFFER THE LITTLE
CHILDREN
TO COME UNTO ME,
AND FORBID THEM NOT:
FOR OF SUCH IS
THE KINGDOM OF GOD.

MARK 10:14B, KJV

Children were often seen as socially insignificant in the first-century Jewish world. Although families cherished their children, they had few rights and little societal status. Roman society idealized childhood in art and literature, while Jewish culture emphasized adulthood as the stage of wisdom and responsibility.

It was unusual for a rabbi to prioritize children, so when Jesus's disciples rebuked the people bringing children to him, they likely did so because they believed Jesus's time was too valuable for such encounters. Religious teachers typically focused on men, scholars, and elders, but Jesus's embrace of children was radical, demonstrating a countercultural emphasis on humility and dependence on God.

Jesus's words, "Of such is the kingdom of God," signified a profound spiritual lesson. He was not merely blessing the children; he made them an example of faith. In Jewish tradition, children depended entirely on their parents, just as Jesus emphasized that believers should depend entirely on God. Children were also closely associated with purity and sincerity in Jewish thought. Jesus's invitation, "Suffer the little children to come unto me," was a declaration that God's kingdom was not about status, intellect, or power, but about trust, openness, and simplicity.

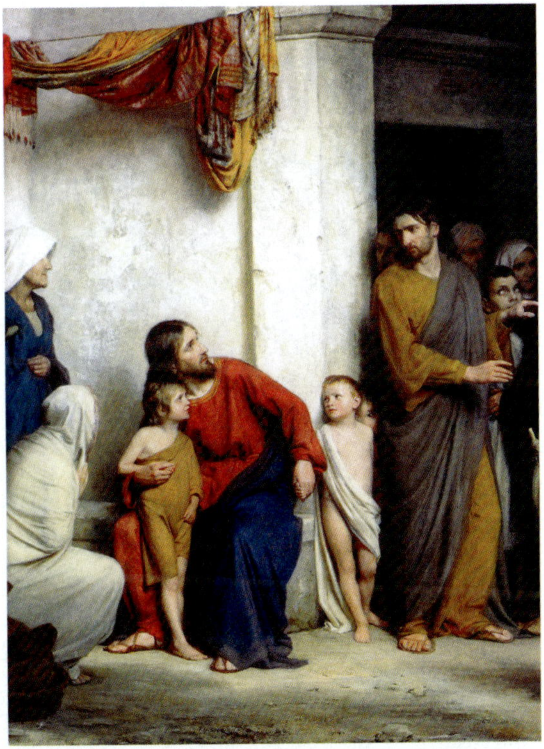

Suffer the Children, Carl Bloch, ca. 1865–1879. Chapel at Frederiksborg Palace, Copenhagen, Denmark.

Jesus did not see the interaction with children as an

imposition to be endured as the word "suffer" might imply to modern readers. The word translated "suffer" comes from a Greek word meaning to "let" or "permit." The fact that Jesus went on to perform the Jewish tradition of laying hands on and speaking a blessing over the children—an act often performed by fathers or priests—demonstrated his care for the most powerless in society. Doing so in a public setting reinforced his role as a spiritual leader who welcomed everyone, regardless of their social standing.

The blessing itself is not recorded but may have paralleled the priestly blessing (Numbers 6:24–26) typically spoken over children on Shabbot and other special occasions: "May you be like Ephraim and Menashe (for boys; or Sarah, Rebekah, Rachel, and Leah for girls). May God bless you and protect you.

Christ Receiving the Children, Sébastien Bourdon, 1655. Art Institute of Chicago, Chicago, Illinois, USA.

May God show you favor and be gracious to you. May God show you kindness and grant you peace." Although specific traditions vary between families, usually the person giving the blessing places one or both hands on the child's head, and the practice contributes to a special feeling of closeness between parents and children.

Blessing the children was also significant within the broader teachings of Jesus on social inclusion. While religious leaders and the elite sought prestige, Jesus elevated people who were considered least in society—children, women, poor people, and outcasts. This act foreshadowed his later rebukes of religious legalism and his radical redefinition of spiritual greatness.

This passage has had a lasting cultural and theological impact, influencing teachings on baptism, childlike faith, and the value of children in God's kingdom and continues to be cited in discussions of Christian parenting, education, and social responsibility today.

WHOSOEVER SHALL
NOT RECEIVE
THE KINGDOM OF GOD
AS A LITTLE CHILD,
HE SHALL NOT ENTER
THEREIN.

MARK 10:15b, KJV

The Greatest Commandment

Matthew 22:36–40

The Pharisees and the Sadducees Come to Tempt Jesus, James Tissot, ca. 1886–1894. Brooklyn Museum, Brooklyn, New York, USA.

THOU SHALT LOVE THE LORD
THY GOD WITH ALL THY HEART,
AND WITH ALL THY SOUL, AND
WITH ALL THY MIND.
THIS IS THE FIRST AND GREAT
COMMANDMENT. AND THE
SECOND IS LIKE UNTO IT,
THOU SHALT LOVE
THY NEIGHBOUR
AS THYSELF.

MATTHEW 22:37–39, KJV

The foundation of Jewish belief and practice, called the *Torah*, is spread among the books of Exodus, Leviticus, Numbers, and Deuteronomy. The regulations are numerous and span moral laws; social laws; food laws; purity laws; rules and instructions regarding feasts, sacrifices, and worship; and instructions regarding the Tabernacle, national leadership, and the responsibilities of the high priest.

Some regulations in the Torah, also called Mosaic Law, are detailed and explicit, while others are vague and open to interpretation. Because many of the rules required interpretation to be put into practice, a large body of additional material—interpretations, traditions, and debates—has accompanied Torah study ever since. Rabbis calculated the total number of commandments in the Torah to be 613.

Jewish religious teachers often debated which of the 613 commandments in the Torah was the most important. When a Pharisee tested Jesus with this question, it was part of an ongoing theological discussion among Jewish scholars. Jesus's response, quoting Deuteronomy 6:5 and Leviticus 19:18, summarized the entire Mosaic Law into two simple yet profound principles: love for God and love for neighbor.

The Nash Papyrus contains a portion of a pre-Masoretic Text, specifically the Ten Commandments and the *Shema Yisrael* prayer, ca.100s BC.

The Pharisees and Sadducees, two dominant Jewish religious groups, interpreted the Torah differently. Pharisees emphasized strict observance of traditions; Sadducees adhered more closely to the written Torah. Jesus's response challenged the legalistic approach of both groups, shifting the focus from ritual obedience to genuine love and compassion.

The first commandment was taken from the *Shema*, the central declaration of Jewish faith recited daily by devout Jews. This commandment emphasized total devotion to God, encompassing a person's thoughts, emotions, and actions. Jesus's teaching around the second commandment was revolutionary, expanding the traditional concept of neighbor beyond ethnic and social boundaries. While Leviticus 19:18 instructed Jews to love their neighbors, some leaders had interpreted "neighbor" narrowly, applying it only to fellow Israelites. Jesus's teaching in the parable of the Good Samaritan (Luke 10:25–37) broadened the definition of "neighbor" to encompass everyone.

Christ Among the Pharisees, Jacob Jordaens, ca. 1660–1670. Private collection.

Similarly, Jesus's prior teaching on love for enemies—"I tell you, love your enemies and pray for those who persecute you" (Matthew 5:44, NIV)—extended the meaning of this commandment even further. Jesus taught that people should always demonstrate love no matter how badly they had been treated. These teachings described a new, higher standard of religious behavior, making it clear that *all people*—friends and foes alike—deserve love and respect.

In Jewish thought, love was not only an emotion, but also an action. Love for God meant obedience to his commandments, and love for neighbor meant practical acts of kindness and justice. Jesus's emphasis on these two commandments anticipated the Golden Rule—"Do to others what you would have them do to you" (Matthew 7:12, NIV)—which became a defining ethic of Christian morality.

Ultimately, Jesus's response to the Pharisee was more than a legal answer—it was a radical redefinition of righteousness. By prioritizing love, Jesus reconciled the law with the heart, calling people to live in a way that reflected God's character rather than mere rule following.

ON THESE TWO
COMMANDMENTS
HANG
ALL THE LAW
AND
THE PROPHETS.

MATTHEW 22:40, KJV

MIRACLES & WONDERS

Calming the Storm

Mark 4:35–41

Christ in the Storm on the Sea of Galilee, Ludolf Bakhuizen, 1695. Indianapolis Museum of Art, Indianapolis, Indiana, USA.

AND HE AROSE,
AND REBUKED THE WIND,
AND SAID UNTO THE SEA,
PEACE, BE STILL.
AND THE WIND CEASED,
AND THERE WAS A GREAT CALM.

MARK 4:39, KJV

Located between one- and two-day's walk from Nazareth, the Sea of Galilee is known for sudden and violent storms due to unique geographical features. This body of water, sometimes called the Lake of Gennesaret, lies about 700 feet *below* sea level making it the lowest freshwater lake on Earth and the second-lowest lake in the world. The hills that surround it act as wind tunnels for strong gusts of cold, dry air from the northeast, generating rapid weather changes during the winter and early spring. Occasionally these wild winds stir up the water in the Galilee basin to significant heights, creating waves more than ten feet high. These storms could be particularly dangerous for small fishing boats, like those used by Jesus and his disciples.

One such storm arose when Jesus and his disciples crossed the lake after a long day of teaching from a boat along its shore. Waves spilled into the boat while Jesus slept on a cushion. The disciples, increasingly anxious about the situation, woke Jesus up to ask if he cared that they are all about to die on a sinking ship.

In the first century, fishing was a primary industry in Galilee, and many of Jesus's disciples were experienced fishermen. They would have been accustomed to the unpredictability of the Sea of Galilee, which makes their fear during the storm recorded in this account even more significant.

"Reference Map of Ancient Palestine" (detail of Galilee), from *The Historical Atlas*, Folio 6-7, William R. Shepherd, published by Henry Holt and Company, 1911.

The storm was clearly severe enough that even these seasoned sailors believed they were in mortal danger.

Yet Jesus remained asleep in the boat, a detail that illustrated both his humanity and a deep trust in God's sovereignty. Once awakened, Jesus rebuked the wind and commanded the sea to be still.

And the wind stopped. And the sea calmed.

The disciples were astonished at what they saw. Jesus asked his disciples why they were afraid; did they still lack faith? But the men asked each other "What manner of man is this, that even the wind and the sea obey him?" (Mark 4:41, KJV), revealing a growing realization of Jesus's divine nature.

This miracle had strong Old Testament parallels, particularly to Psalm 107:28–29, which described sailors crying out to God in distress and God calming the storm. Jesus's actions mirrored God's authority over nature, foreshadowing the claim that he was the Son of God. This moment would have had profound implications for his disciples, many of whom were still grasping the full scope of his divine mission.

Jesus on the Lake of Gennesaret, Alexandre-Gabriel Decamps, ca. 1850–1875. Louvre Museum, Paris, France.

Additionally, ancient Jewish thought often associated chaotic waters with evil forces. The deep sea was sometimes seen as a symbol of chaos and opposition to God's order (Genesis 1:2; Job 38:8–11). By calming the storm, Jesus not only rescued his disciples but demonstrated his power over the forces of nature and chaos.

This event deeply impacted the disciples, preparing them for future trials where they would need to trust in Jesus amid life's storms. The miracle was not just about physical deliverance, but also about teaching them a lesson in faith—to rely on God even in the most turbulent times.

WHAT MANNER OF MAN IS THIS, THAT EVEN THE WIND AND THE SEA OBEY HIM?

MARK 4:41, KJV

Feeding the 5,000

John 6:1–15

Feeding the Five Thousand, John Martin, ca. 1789–1854. Yale Center for British Art, New Haven, Connecticut, USA.

"THERE IS A BOY HERE
WHO HAS FIVE BARLEY LOAVES
AND TWO FISH, BUT WHAT ARE
THEY FOR SO MANY?" . . .
JESUS THEN TOOK THE
LOAVES, AND WHEN HE
HAD GIVEN THANKS,
HE DISTRIBUTED THEM TO
THOSE WHO WERE SEATED.
SO ALSO THE FISH,
AS MUCH AS THEY WANTED.

JOHN 6:9, 11, ESV

Hospitality has been an important custom in the Middle East from ancient times. Providing food for guests would have been viewed as a sacred obligation in the first-century Jewish world. One day while Jesus was teaching his disciples in a place near Bethsaida on the northern shore of the Sea of Galilee, crowds arrived that had been following Jesus because he had been healing the sick.

The day grew late, but the crowds stayed. The mountainous terrain and remoteness of the location contributed to concern about how such a vast group could be fed. Faced with the challenge of feeding 5,000 men, plus women and children, Jesus asked Philip where they could buy food. His question was rhetorical, emphasizing the impossibility of the task—no nearby markets could provide such an amount, nor did the group have sufficient money to purchase enough food even if it had been available.

Hills of Galilee, John Singer Sargent, 1905–1906. Brooklyn Museum, Brooklyn, New York, USA.

Andrew, another disciple, pointed out a boy carrying five barley loaves and two fish, likely part of a simple meal for the boy and his family. Jesus blessed the boy's food, broke the bread, and distributed it to a crowd some scholars estimate was closer to 15,000 people. Stunningly, the boy's miniscule amount fed the entire group with food to spare.

This miraculous multiplication of food evoked Old Testament parallels, including God providing manna in the wilderness (Exodus 16:4–35) and Elisha feeding 100 men with 20 loaves of bread (2 Kings 4:42–44). The emphasis on 12 baskets of leftovers symbolized God's abundant provision and the twelve tribes of Israel, linking this event to Israel's spiritual nourishment.

The region around the Sea of Galilee was heavily populated with both Jewish and Gentile communities, making this miracle an inclusive sign of Jesus's mission to all people. The fact that the crowd sought to make Jesus their king afterward (John 6:15) shows they were actively awaiting a messianic leader who would restore Israel's independence from Rome. However, Jesus rejected this political interpretation of his mission and instead withdrew from the crowd to pray alone.

Feeding the 5,000 is one of the few miracles recorded in all four Gospels, which underscores its significance in Jesus's ministry. It also introduced the

Mosaic tile floor depicting loaves and fishes at the reported site of Jesus feeding 5,000, unknown artist, ca. AD 480. Church of the Multiplication, Tabgha, Israel.

theme of Jesus as the "Bread of Life," on which he later expounded: "Whoever comes to me shall not hunger, and whoever believes in me shall never thirst" (John 6:35).

This feeding miracle was not merely about physical sustenance, but also about spiritual nourishment, pointing toward the coming Eucharistic tradition in Christian theology. The location of the miracle, believed to be at Tabgha, remains a significant pilgrimage site today. The Church of the Multiplication, built there in the fifth century, features ancient mosaics depicting loaves and fish, reinforcing the enduring power of this event in Christian memory.

SO THEY GATHERED THEM UP AND FILLED TWELVE BASKETS WITH FRAGMENTS FROM THE FIVE BARLEY LOAVES LEFT BY THOSE WHO HAD EATEN.

JOHN 6:13, ESV

WALKING ON WATER

Matthew 14:22–33

Man of Sorrows, William Dyce, ca. 1860. National Galleries of Scotland, Edinburgh, Scotland, UK.

"LORD, IF IT'S YOU,"
PETER REPLIED,
"TELL ME TO
COME TO YOU ON THE WATER."
"COME,"
HE SAID. THEN PETER GOT
DOWN OUT OF THE BOAT,
WALKED ON THE WATER
AND CAME TOWARD JESUS.

MATTHEW 14:28–29, NIV

Shortly after the stunning event of feeding 5,000 men (plus women and children) who gathered to hear Jesus teach with two fish and five loaves of bread, he sent his disciples ahead by boat to their next destination, likely Capernaum, while he stayed behind to pray alone on the mountainside.

While it's impossible to know with certainty the exact sequence of events, both Matthew and Mark's Gospels indicate this occurred not long after Jesus's cousin, John the Baptist, was brutally beheaded at the command of Herod Antipas, tetrarch of Galilee under Caesar Augustus (Matthew 14:12–14; Mark 6:29–34). The Gospel accounts seem to imply that Jesus likely sought solitude to grieve and pray but had been interrupted by the gathering crowds that he then fed miraculously. It was after this that Jesus finally withdrew into solitude. Jesus's actions that night reflected common Jewish traditions where prophets and leaders often sought isolation to commune with God, as Moses did on Mount Sinai (Exodus 19:20).

Jesus stayed alone on the mountain for most of the night, giving ample time for the experienced fishermen to travel quite a distance away from shore on the Sea of Galilee, a freshwater lake about 13 miles long and eight miles wide. Mark records that during the fourth watch of the night (Mark 6:48), which was between 3:00 and 6:00 a.m., the disciples saw a shocking image: Jesus walking toward them on the tumultuous stormy water.

The Disciples See Christ Walking on the Water, Henry Ossawa Tanner, 1907. Des Moines Art Center, Des Moines, Iowa, USA.

The disciples were terrified. This was so far out of their experience that they believed they were seeing a ghost, a common first-century belief about spirits and supernatural entities appearing over water. In ancient Jewish thought, the sea symbolized chaos and the unknown and walking on it signified divine authority.

Jesus's response, "Be of good cheer; it is I; be not afraid" (Matthew 14:27, KJV), echoes Old Testament occurrences where God reassured his people with his presence. The phrase "It is I" (Greek: *ego eimi*) mirrored God's self-identification to Moses at the burning bush (Exodus 3:14) and reinforced Jesus's divine identity.

Then Peter did something bold: He got out of the boat to walk to Jesus. Shockingly, Peter didn't sink until he paid attention to the wind and waves and was afraid. When he began to sink, he cried, "Lord, save me!" Jesus immediately reached out, saved him, and chided Peter's wavering faith.

Christ at the Sea of Galilee, likely Lambert Sustris, ca. 1570–1575. National Gallery of Art, Washington, DC, USA.

When Jesus and Peter reentered the boat, the storm ceased immediately, leading the disciples to worship him and declare, "Truly you are the Son of God" (Matthew 14:32, KJV). This is the first recorded instance of the disciples openly acknowledging Jesus's divine nature, and it parallels Psalm 107:29, which describes God as the one who "stilled the storm to a whisper" (KJV).

This miracle demonstrated Jesus's authority over nature, reinforcing his divine power. It also illustrated the necessity of faith, as seen in Peter's experience. This event would later serve as a foundational moment in Christian theology, symbolizing unwavering trust in Jesus amid life's storms.

BUT WHEN [PETER] SAW THE WIND,
HE WAS AFRAID
AND, BEGINNING TO SINK,
CRIED OUT, "LORD, SAVE ME!"
IMMEDIATELY JESUS
REACHED OUT HIS HAND
AND CAUGHT HIM.
"YOU OF LITTLE FAITH," HE SAID,
"WHY DID YOU DOUBT?"

MATTHEW 14:30–31, NIV

Healing the Physically Ill Woman

Mark 5:25–34

Christ Healing the Blind, Philippe de Champaigne, ca. 1655–1660. Timken Museum of Art, San Diego, California, USA.

SHE THOUGHT,
"IF I JUST TOUCH HIS CLOTHES,
I WILL BE HEALED."
IMMEDIATELY HER BLEEDING
STOPPED AND SHE FELT IN HER
BODY THAT SHE WAS FREED
FROM HER SUFFERING.

MARK 5:28–29, NIV

At a time when Greeks and Romans gave offerings at their temples in exchange for healing, Jesus healed people free of charge wherever he encountered a need. He performed this ministry often at considerable risk to himself. The Gospels of Matthew, Mark, Luke, and John provide 41 stories of individual physical or mental healing.

In one such story, Jesus was once again surrounded by a crush of people. At the edge of the crowd was a woman who had suffered from chronic bleeding for twelve years, a condition that made her ritually unclean according to Jewish purity laws (Leviticus 15:25–27). This meant that she was ostracized from society, barred from public worship, and unable to have physical contact with other people, because anyone who touched her would also become unclean.

The social stigma surrounding such an illness was immense. Women's roles in first-century Jewish society were already limited. They were considered second-class persons and as such were forbidden from talking to strangers, testifying in court, or from leaving their homes without the permission of their fathers or husbands. This woman was further isolated by her condition, likely leaving her without support or companionship. She had spent all her money on physicians, but rather than being healed,

Mark 5:22-34. On the Way to the House of Jairus, William Hole, 1846–1917. Library of Congress, Washington, DC, USA.

her condition worsened. In ancient times, medical treatments were often rudimentary, and women had limited access to effective healthcare.

Her decision to touch Jesus's cloak was an act of bold faith, but it also violated Jewish purity laws. According to tradition, anyone she touched would become ritually unclean. However, she believed that even touching Jesus's garment would be enough to heal her. This belief was not unusual—many people in the ancient world ascribed power to the clothing of holy men. The hem of Jesus's garment may have referred to the *tzitzit* (Hebrew for tassels) of his prayer shawl, which were significant in Jewish tradition as a reminder of God's commandments (Numbers 15:38–40).

The moment she touched Jesus's garment she was instantly healed. Jesus, aware of what had transpired, asked, "Who touched me?" His disciples, perplexed by the crowded surroundings, did not understand why he asked this question. But the account seems to imply that Jesus wanted to acknowledge her faith publicly, not just heal her in secret.

The Healing of a Bleeding Woman, fresco by unknown artist, ca. AD 301–400. Catacombs of Marcellinus and Peter, Rome, Italy.

When the woman came forward in fear, Jesus did not rebuke her but instead affirmed her faith, saying, "Daughter, your faith has healed you." His use of the word *daughter* is significant. It is the only recorded time that Jesus addresses someone this way, signifying acceptance and restoration into the community. He did not only heal her physically but also restored her socially and spiritually.

This profound story of faith, desperation, and divine restoration highlights Jesus's compassion and disregard for social and ritual barriers. By healing this woman, he not only defied purity laws, but also demonstrated that faith, rather than legalistic restrictions, was what truly connected people to God. Many people today continue to see this woman's healing as a powerful example that no one is too isolated or unworthy to receive God's regard.

DAUGHTER,
YOUR FAITH HAS HEALED YOU.
GO IN PEACE AND BE FREED
FROM YOUR SUFFERING.

MARK 5:34, NIV

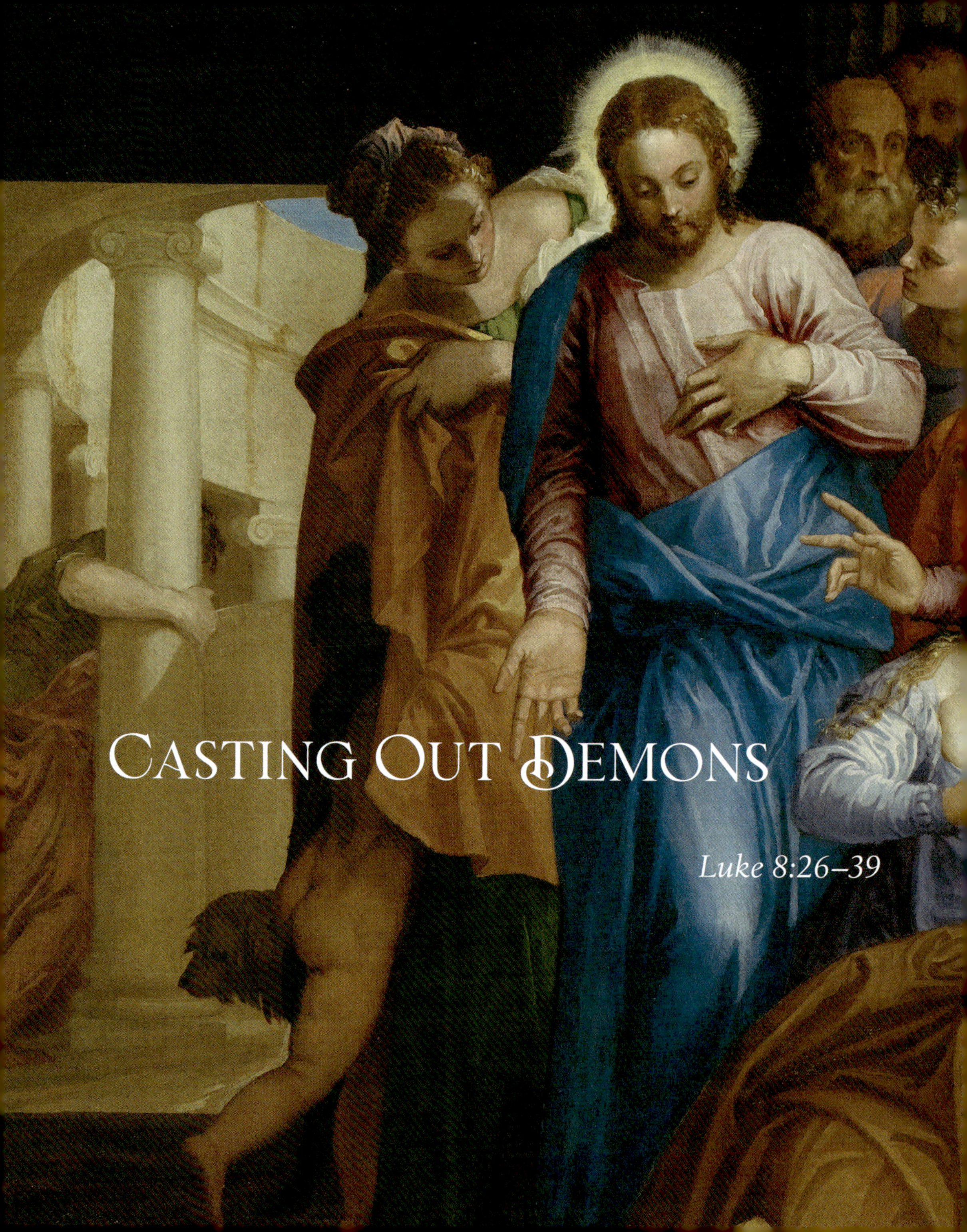

Casting Out Demons

Luke 8:26–39

The Conversion of Mary Magdalene, Paolo Veronese, ca. 1548. National Gallery, London, England, UK.

THEY CAME TO JESUS
AND FOUND THE MAN
FROM WHOM THE DEMONS
HAD GONE,
SITTING AT THE FEET OF JESUS,
CLOTHED AND
IN HIS RIGHT MIND.

LUKE 8:35, ESV

In addition to healing people from a multitude of illnesses throughout his itinerant ministry, Jesus was recorded as casting out demons numerous times. Demon possession was a recurring element in the Gospel accounts, often serving as the dramatic setting for some of Jesus's most vivid miracles.

Some physical conditions in first-century Judea were seen through a spiritual lens rather than a medical one. Afflictions such as seizures, blindness, or sudden violent outbursts were often attributed to unclean spirits. Jesus's authority over these afflictions no matter their cause was one of the key signs of his divine identity in the Gospels. He didn't just heal physical illnesses; he restored mental and spiritual health, often in public view, with commands such as "Come out of him!" and "Be silent!"

One of the most personally significant of these stories was the deliverance of Mary Magdalene, who most likely grew up on the western shore of Galilee in the village of Magdala. Two Gospel writers recorded that Jesus cast out seven demons from her (Mark 16:9; Luke 8:2), setting her apart as someone profoundly touched by Jesus's healing power.

Christ Healing a Lunatic and Judas Receiving Thirty Pieces of Silver, (detail), Francesco d'Antonio di Bartolomeo, ca. 1425–1426. Philadelphia Museum of Art, Philadelphia, Pennsylvania, USA.

That miraculous experience converted a once-troubled woman into a faithful follower. According to Luke, Mary Magdalene was among the women healed from "evil spirits and infirmities" who accompanied Jesus on his ministry journeys and listed alongside Joanna and Susanna as a financial supporter of Jesus's ministry—a striking role in a patriarchal society (Luke 8:2–3). All four Gospel writers frequently highlighted the radical inclusion of women—particularly a woman such as Mary who was formerly afflicted by demons—as respected members of Jesus's traveling circle. It was an important indicator of how his ministry inverted social norms.

Mary Magdalene's transformation would have been widely recognized by people in the community. In a culture where spiritual purity and status were intertwined, her full restoration and elevated role would have seemed scandalous to everyone and religious leaders in particular—yet Jesus continually defied such expectations. Importantly, her deliverance from demonic torment became the backdrop for her prominence in later Christian tradition as the "apostle to the apostles."

"The Exorcism," from *Très Riches Heures du duc de Berry*, Folio 166r, Limbourg Brothers, ca. 1412–1416. Condé Museum, Chantilly, France.

Beyond Mary Magdalene, Jesus was reported to have cast out demons on numerous occasions: including the Gerasene demoniac (Luke 8:26–39), a mute man (Matthew 9:32–34), a boy with seizures (Mark 9:14–29), and others. His repeated exorcisms pointed not only to a ministry of healing but to a spiritual war being waged. The Gospel writers often framed these encounters as cosmic showdowns where Jesus asserted power over forces of darkness. The demons themselves often recognized Jesus first and spoke to his divine identity: "What have we to do with thee, Jesus, thou Son of God?" (Matthew 8:29, KJV).

At the end of his ministry, Jesus commissioned his disciples to continue casting out demons (Mark 16:17), underscoring that spiritual liberation was to remain a core function of the Christian mission. These dramatic deliverances were not incidental—they set the stage for a broader understanding of salvation that was personal and social as well as spiritual.

AND HE WENT AWAY,
PROCLAIMING
THROUGHOUT THE WHOLE CITY
HOW MUCH JESUS HAD
DONE FOR HIM.

LUKE 8:39b, ESV

Raising People from the Dead

John 11:1–44

The Raising of Jairus's Daughter, George Percy Jacomb-Hood, 1895. Guildhall Art Gallery, London, England, UK.

I AM
THE RESURRECTION
AND THE LIFE.
WHOEVER BELIEVES
IN ME, THOUGH HE DIE,
YET SHALL HE LIVE,
AND EVERYONE WHO
LIVES AND BELIEVES IN ME
SHALL NEVER DIE.

JOHN 11:25–26, ESV

The Gospels record three instances of Jesus raising people from the dead. When Jesus healed the woman who had suffered from chronic bleeding, he was on his way to help Jairus's 12-year-old daughter (Mark 5:21–24). While Jesus was healing the woman, word came that Jairus's daughter had just died, but Jesus reassured the distraught father and claimed she was only sleeping.

Jesus proceeded to bring her back to life privately and then insisted on secrecy from her parents and the disciples with him. It is unclear why Jesus did this (Mark 5:35–43), but his desire for secrecy was overrun when he encountered the widow of Nain burying her only son and had compassion for her (Luke 7:11–17). Her son, who was her sole support, would have been dead for a short time, as burials were to take place within 24 hours. Without him, she faced a bleak future without resources.

But the account of Lazarus is even more dramatic. Jesus was close friends with Lazarus and his sisters, Mary and Martha, who lived in Bethany, a village near Jerusalem. When Lazarus fell gravely ill, the sisters sent word to Jesus. They were confident Jesus would come heal their brother. But Jesus delayed. In fact, John said Jesus did that intentionally so that his disciples would believe (John 11:14–15).

"Jesus Raises a Widow's Son at Nain," from illuminated and illustrated Arabic *Gospels* created in Egypt, Folio 157A, Ilyas Basim Khuri Bazzi Rahib, 1684. Walters Art Museum, Baltimore, Maryland, USA.

When Jesus finally arrived four days after Lazarus was in the tomb, Martha and Mary were understandably grief-stricken and hurt that he had not come sooner. Then in a moment of profound humanity, Jesus wept (John 11:35). He wept even knowing what he would do next. When Jesus raised Lazarus from death back to life, everyone present was deeply moved. This act solidified Jesus's reputation for holding divine power over life and death. It also triggered strong reactions in the religious leaders who began formally discussing how to silence Jesus by killing him (John 11:47–53). Lazarus's resurrection became the turning point that hastened the path to Jesus's crucifixion.

The Raising of Lazarus (after Rembrandt), Vincent van Gogh, 1890. Van Gogh Museum, Amsterdam, Netherlands.

Raising the dead was an uncommon claim in the ancient world. Although miraculous healing and divine intervention appear in both Jewish and Greco-Roman traditions, resurrection was exceedingly rare. In first-century Judea, many Jews believed in a future general resurrection of the dead at the end of time, as mentioned by Martha (John 11:24). However, the idea of an individual being brought back to life before the end times was unprecedented and would have signaled either an extraordinary divine endorsement or heretical sorcery.

Lazarus's resurrection foreshadowed Jesus's own. It acted as a demonstration of Jesus's authority over death and a preview of what was to come. While Lazarus was resuscitated to his former life, Eastern tradition says he eventually died again after serving as bishop of Cyprus, where he likely immigrated to escape potential execution plotted by religious leaders in Jerusalem (John 12:9–11). In comparison, Jesus's resurrection was described as a transformation into an eternal, glorified state. The Lazarus account therefore bridged the human experience of grief and loss with the hope of divine restoration.

MANY OF THE JEWS
THEREFORE,
WHO HAD COME WITH MARY
AND HAD SEEN WHAT HE DID,
BELIEVED IN HIM.

JOHN 11:45, ESV

The Road to the Cross & Resurrection

Jesus's Triumphal Entry

Matthew 21:1–11

Entry of the Christ in Jerusalem, Jean-Léon Gérôme, 1897. Musée Georges-Garret, Vesoul, France.

HOSANNA

TO THE SON OF DAVID:

BLESSED IS HE

THAT COMETH IN

THE NAME OF THE LORD;

HOSANNA

IN THE HIGHEST.

MATTHEW 21:9, KJV

It was Passover again, a deeply significant holiday commemorating the Israelites' liberation from Egyptian bondage. Jerusalem was crowded with people, and the city's atmosphere was likely tense with religious fervor and political expectations. But despite the danger of the religious leaders plotting to kill him, Jesus and his disciples made their way to Jerusalem with the rest of the pilgrims.

When they neared the Mount of Olives, Jesus unexpectedly sent two disciples into the village of Bethphage to borrow a donkey and her colt, telling them where the animal would be and what to say if they were questioned. Surprisingly, the

Christ's Entry into Jerusalem, fresco in southern transept of Lower Basilica, Pietro Lorenzetti, ca. 1310–1329. Basilica of Saint Francis of Assisi, Assisi, Italy.

event unfolded exactly as Jesus predicted. The disciples then put cloaks on the donkey, and Jesus rode the approximately three miles to Jerusalem while the gathered crowd laid down palm branches and their own cloaks to herald his arrival.

The laying of palm branches and garments on the road was a gesture of homage often reserved for royalty. Palm branches symbolized victory and were part of Jewish national identity, especially during previous revolts like the Maccabean revolt commemorated at Hanukkah. The crowd's actions recalled earlier triumphal entries, but Jesus's peaceful demeanor stood in stark contrast to previous traditions.

According to the Gospel of Matthew, Jesus deliberately orchestrated his entrance to echo a prophecy from Zechariah to signal both kingship and peace (Zechariah 9:9). The prophet Zechariah had foretold a future king who would come not on a warhorse but on a humble donkey, signaling a reign not of conquest but of peace and righteousness. This was a conscious contrast to the displays of military prowess typical of Roman or even earlier Jewish monarchs. The tension between royal symbolism and humble demeanor was a deliberate theological and political provocation.

Reconstruction of Jerusalem and the Temple of Herod, James Tissot, ca. 1886–1894. Brooklyn Museum, Brooklyn, New York, USA.

Jesus's method of entry directly challenged the people's political and religious expectations. Many among the crowds saw in Jesus the potential fulfillment of their hopes for a Messiah—a political liberator who would drive out the Roman occupiers and restore national independence. Their cries of "Hosanna to the son of David" were laden with nationalistic meaning. *Hosanna* is derived from a Hebrew phrase meaning "save us," and "son of David" invoked a royal lineage, connecting Jesus to Israel's most revered king and signaling messianic hopes.

Yet, as the Gospel narrative makes clear, this acclaim was not universal. The religious authorities in Jerusalem viewed Jesus with growing alarm. His popularity with the crowds, his prophetic critiques, and his symbolic actions in the Temple—like overturning the tables of the money changers (Matthew 21:12)—threatened both their influence and the fragile political balance they maintained with Roman authorities.

His entry into Jerusalem was pivotal because it marked the beginning of the final week of his earthly ministry and initiated the rapid series of events leading to Jesus's arrest, trial, crucifixion, and—according to Christian belief—his resurrection. Jesus's triumphal entry served as both declaration and confrontation: he claimed kingship in a new kind of kingdom—one built on humility, justice, and spiritual renewal.

SEE, YOUR KING
COMES TO YOU, . . .
LOWLY AND RIDING ON
A DONKEY, ON A COLT,
THE FOAL OF A DONKEY.

ZECHARIAH 9:9, NIV

THE LAST SUPPER

Luke 22:7–23

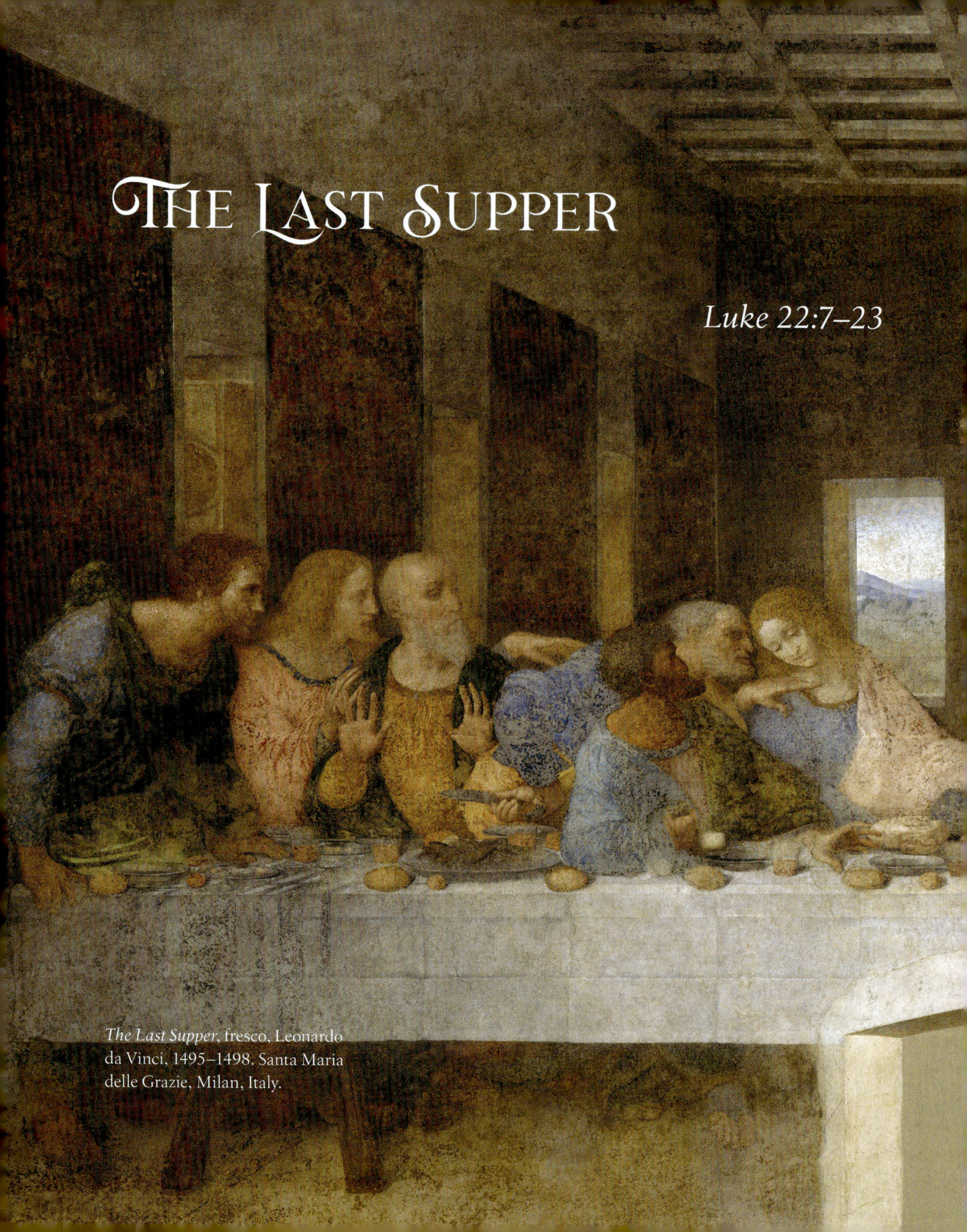

The Last Supper, fresco, Leonardo da Vinci, 1495–1498. Santa Maria delle Grazie, Milan, Italy.

AND HE TOOK BREAD,
AND GAVE THANKS,
AND BRAKE IT, AND
GAVE UNTO THEM,
SAYING, THIS IS MY BODY
WHICH IS GIVEN FOR YOU:
THIS DO IN
REMEMBRANCE OF ME.

LUKE 22:19, KJV

Despite an action-packed week and imminent threat to his life, Jesus gathered with his disciples in Jerusalem for the Passover festival, an annual weeklong celebration deeply rooted in Jewish identity that commemorated the Israelites' emancipation from Egyptian slavery.

Jesus sent Peter and John into Jerusalem to prepare the Passover Seder, a fifteen-step, ritual-packed feast that would have included slaughtering the Passover lamb and preparing unleavened bread. The lamb symbolizes the final night before the Israelites were released from slavery, when they painted their doorposts with the blood of an unblemished lamb to protect all within from the angel of death, which killed all the firstborn in Egypt. Unleavened bread is consumed because the Israelites did not have time for their bread to rise before fleeing the Egyptians.

Once the meal was prepared, Jesus and his disciples shared the meal in an upper room. They likely reclined on low couches around a table in keeping with the customs of Greco-Roman dining during festive occasions. Jesus expressed to his disciples that he had eagerly desired to share this meal with them, suggesting a deep awareness of its symbolic weight.

What made the Last Supper so significant, though, was Jesus's bold reinterpretation of the Passover elements. He took the *matzah*—unleavened

Christ Washing the Feet of His Disciples, Jacopo Tintoretto, ca. 1547. Museo del Prado, Madrid, Spain.

bread—and declared, "This is my body, which is given for you." Matzah is traditionally broken before reciting the story of the Exodus and eaten with bitter herbs in a ritual portion before the meal.

Similarly, Jesus held the cup of wine after supper and pronounced, "This cup is the new testament in my blood, which is shed for you." There are four cups of wine or grape juice consumed during the Passover seder: the Cup of Sanctification, drunk at the beginning of the meal as a declaration of freedom; the Cup of Plagues, drunk after the recital of the escape from Egypt, representing deliverance; the Cup of Redemption, drunk after the meal, symbolizing the coming of Messiah; and the Cup of Praise, drunk at the end of the seder, representing the acceptance of God's people. Jesus's reframing of the symbolism of

The Last Supper, Pieter Pourbus, 1548. Groeninge Museum, Bruges, Belgium.

the bread and wine with his own imminent death marked a pivotal moment and infused the Passover with radical new meaning for his followers.

John's Gospel further amplified this symbolism by drawing a parallel between Jesus and the Passover lamb, which was required to be without blemish (Exodus 12:5). Early Christian communities saw Jesus as the fulfillment of this image. Just as the original Passover lamb's blood marked the deliverance of the Israelites, Jesus's followers came to believe his blood offered liberation from spiritual bondage.

This powerful reinterpretation of tradition laid the groundwork for what would become a central ritual in Christian worship: the Eucharist or Holy Communion. Rooted in the Jewish experience of deliverance, it took on a new dimension as a ritual remembrance of Jesus's sacrifice and reflected the continuity and transformation at the heart of Jesus's message: drawing from sacred memory while pointing toward a new spiritual horizon.

LIKEWISE
ALSO THE CUP AFTER
SUPPER, SAYING, THIS CUP IS
THE NEW TESTAMENT
IN MY BLOOD,
WHICH IS
SHED FOR YOU.

LUKE 22:20, KJV

The Crucifixion

Luke 23:32–49

Christ Carrying the Cross, Titian, 1565.
Museo del Prado, Madrid, Spain.

THEN JESUS, CALLING OUT
WITH A LOUD VOICE, SAID,
"FATHER,
INTO YOUR HANDS
I COMMIT MY SPIRIT!"
AND HAVING SAID THIS HE
BREATHED HIS LAST.

LUKE 23:46, ESV

After a devastating betrayal by a disciple and a series of encounters before cultural, religious, and political leaders, Jesus was led away to be crucified. Most historians believe this took place around AD 30; it is mentioned by both the Roman historian Tacitus and the Jewish historian Josephus.

Roman crucifixion was a public, humiliating form of execution used primarily for slaves, rebels, and criminals. Victims were initially flogged, weakening them significantly before they were forced to carry the horizontal beam of their cross to the place of execution. Golgotha, meaning "Place of the Skull," was the site just outside Jerusalem where Jesus was crucified between two criminals, positioning him as the worst offender. Victims were stripped naked, nailed onto their cross with seven-inch nails, and then hung directly beside the road as a cautionary example to passersby. In an unusual move, a sign was nailed above Jesus's head, reading "King of the Jews" in Aramaic, Latin, and Greek, which was intended as a vicious mockery.

Night at Golgotha, Vasily Petrovich Vereshchagin, 1869. State Tretyakov Gallery, Moscow, Russia.

Eyewitnesses that day included Roman soldiers, Jewish leaders, passersby, some of Jesus's disciples, and a group of female followers among whom was Mary, Jesus's mother. John noted the moment when Jesus, as Mary's oldest son, entrusted Mary's care to a disciple (John 19:25–27). No mention was made of Mary's husband, Joseph, and it is believed he died prior to Jesus beginning his public ministry.

Darkness fell from noon to 3 p.m., a detail reported in all four Gospels. As Jesus endured physical torment, he spoke seven phrases, including prayers, a declaration of thirst, a cry of abandonment, and ultimately, "It is finished." Interestingly Jesus died more quickly than was typical for crucifixion victims, so a soldier pierced his side with a spear producing a flow of blood and water—a sign of death (John 19:33–34).

The moment Jesus died, the curtain in the Temple separating the Holy of Holies from the rest of the sanctuary was torn in two. This dramatic sign suggested Jesus was indeed God's Son and was believed to indicate a new accessibility to God no longer mediated by priests or ritual. Matthew's account even described an earthquake and opening tombs (Matthew 27:51–53), possibly indicating that death itself was shaken. And the Roman centurion overseeing the execution was quoted in multiple Gospels as recognizing something extraordinary: "Truly this man was the Son of God" (Matthew 27:54). This declaration from a Gentile soldier echoed the recurring theme of Jesus's message expanding beyond traditional boundaries.

The Crucifixion (detail, soldier on horseback), unknown Netherlandish artist, ca. 1520. Gemäldegalerie, Berlin, Germany.

Jesus's crucifixion was a climactic turning point of the Christian story. All four Gospels described the event, each adding distinctive details. Although they recorded crucifixion's physical brutality, their accounts were relatively restrained compared to descriptions in other ancient texts and focused more on what the experience revealed about Jesus's identity and mission. Jesus remained stunningly composed, compassionate, and faithful throughout—even forgiving the people who crucified him. This event stands as a profound moment of paradox: apparent defeat becoming the doorway to victory, and suffering transformed into salvation.

NOW WHEN THE CENTURION SAW WHAT HAD TAKEN PLACE, HE PRAISED GOD, SAYING, "CERTAINLY THIS MAN WAS INNOCENT!"

LUKE 23:47, ESV

Jesus's Burial

John 19:38–42

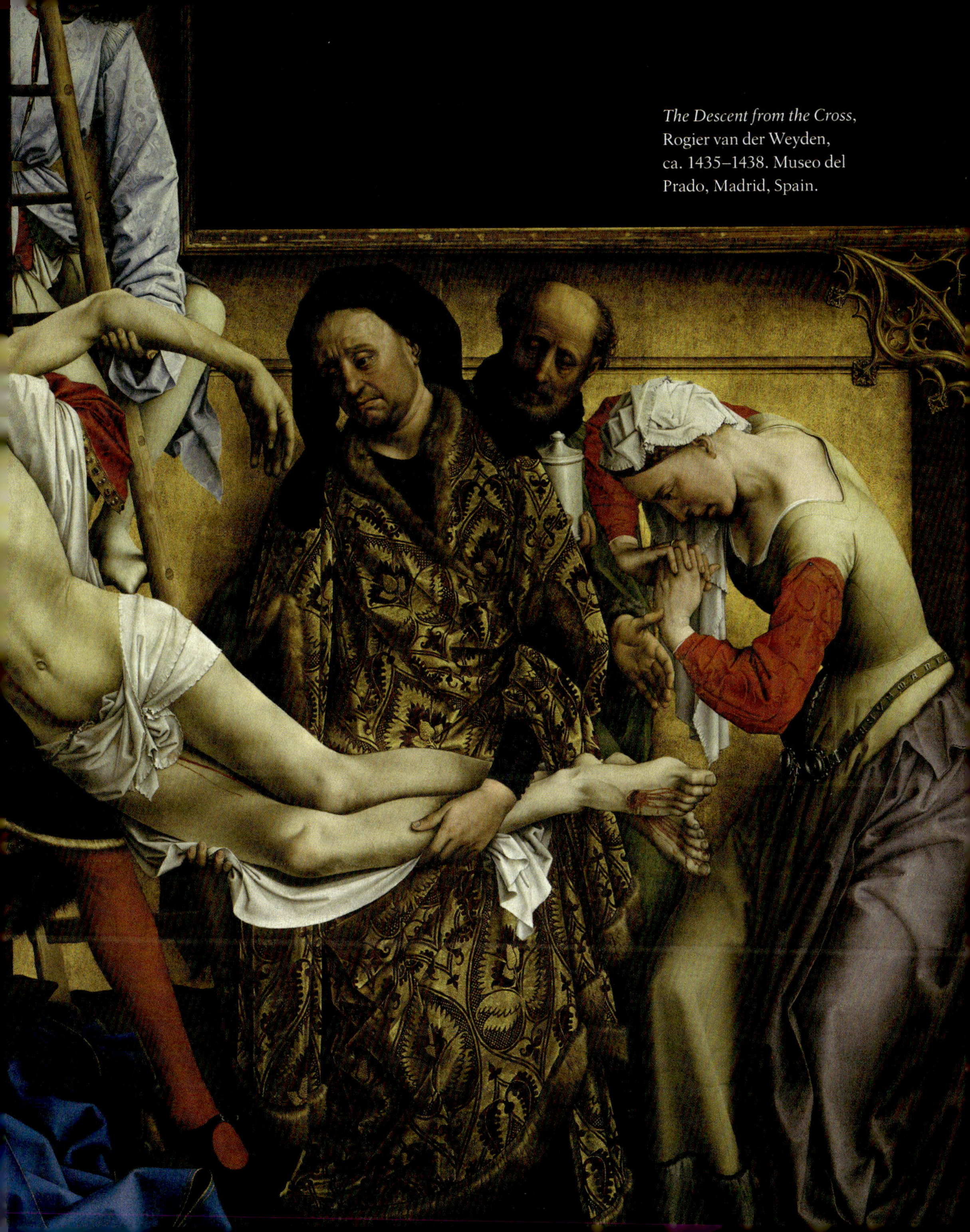

The Descent from the Cross, Rogier van der Weyden, ca. 1435–1438. Museo del Prado, Madrid, Spain.

THEN TOOK THEY
THE BODY OF JESUS, AND
WOUND IT IN LINEN CLOTHES
WITH THE SPICES,
AS THE MANNER OF THE JEWS
IS TO BURY.

JOHN 19:40, KJV

After the brutal finality of Jesus's crucifixion, it grew late in the day. The Sabbath would begin in a few short hours at sundown, bringing urgency to the need to bury the body beforehand. Although Roman custom typically left crucified bodies exposed as a warning to others, Jesus's burial took place with surprising speed.

Joseph of Arimathea, a respected member of the Sanhedrin council who had not supported its decision to condemn Jesus, courageously approached Pontius Pilate and requested the body. His request alone was risky, because it publicly identified him with a man executed for sedition. Pilate, after confirming that Jesus was indeed dead, allowed the request.

Pietà du Château d'Ecouen, Rosso Fiorentino, 1537–1540. Louvre Museum, Paris, France.

Nicodemus, a Jewish leader who had secretly asked Jesus questions, joined Joseph. The two men wrapped Jesus's body in linen cloths and added a large quantity of burial spices—myrrh and aloes—honoring him in a way typically reserved for wealthy or highly esteemed Jews. Their actions, done quietly and respectfully, reflected not only courage but deep reverence.

They placed Jesus's body in a garden tomb near the site of the crucifixion. This tomb, unused and newly cut from rock, belonged to Joseph himself (Matthew 27:60). Its proximity allowed for their haste without sacrificing dignity. A large stone was rolled across the entrance to close the tomb.

All four Gospel accounts emphasized the presence of women who watched the burial from a distance. These women—Mary Magdalene, Mary the mother of James, and others—observed where Jesus was laid so they could return after the Sabbath to anoint the body more thoroughly.

Although Jesus was buried, the story did not rest quietly. Aware of Jesus's prediction that he would rise on the third day, religious leaders were concerned his disciples might steal the body and claim a resurrection, so they approached Pontius Pilate to request that the tomb be secured. Pilate assigned a four-man Roman guard and authorized them to seal the stone. This likely involved a

Sketch for the Chapel of the Sorbonne: Christ in the Tomb, Louis Charles Timbal, 1870–1875. Petit Palais, Paris, France.

cord, stretched across the entrance stone, fastened with wax or clay bearing the Roman seal. Tampering with it was a direct offense against Roman authority with perilous consequences. The trained soldiers, capable of using force, posted at the site were also a serious deterrent.

Ironically, the very precautions meant to suppress any talk of resurrection added layers of credibility to later resurrection reports. The presence of guards, the seal, and the public knowledge of these measures countered the narrative that Jesus's body was stolen or moved in secret. By attempting to block any possibility of deception, the authorities inadvertently gave more weight to what followed.

Matthew's Gospel was the only one to record the efforts of the religious leaders to safeguard the tomb, possibly because of his audience's concern for legal and prophetic fulfillment. In an account that highlighted the intersection of political power, religious anxiety, and divine mystery, Roman guards became an essential part of Jesus's story—not as a footnote, but as an unwitting witness to the power of God.

THERE LAID THEY JESUS THEREFORE BECAUSE OF THE JEWS' PREPARATION DAY; FOR THE SEPULCHRE WAS NIGH AT HAND.

JOHN 19:42, KJV

The Resurrection of Jesus

Matthew 28:1–10

An Angel Opens the Grave of Christ, Benjamin Gerritszoon Cuyp, ca. 1630–1649. Dordrechts Museum, Dordrecht, Netherlands.

HE IS NOT HERE:
FOR HE IS RISEN,
AS HE SAID.
COME, SEE THE PLACE
WHERE THE LORD LAY.

MATTHEW 28:6, KJV

Jesus of Nazareth was dead. Buried. While it was still dark in the early hours before dawn on the first day of the week, the same women who witnessed Jesus's crucifixion and burial returned to his tomb with grief-stricken yet devoted hearts.

Spices in hand, their purpose was clear: anoint the body properly. They had not performed this customary task earlier, because tradition required it be completed before the Sabbath began at sundown, which had occurred shortly after Jesus's death. Approaching the tomb, they worried about who would remove the stone blocking its entrance (Mark 16:3).

But the stone was rolled away and the tomb was empty! How could this be?

The Three Women on the Tomb of Christ, Irma Martin, 1843. Private collection.

All four Gospel accounts, while slightly different in their details, unmistakably recorded women as the first witnesses of Jesus's resurrection. In Matthew's account, the women then encountered both an angel and then Jesus himself, who greeted them with peace and reassurance. John noted that he and Peter ran to the tomb after hearing from Mary Magdalene, but they only saw empty grave clothes in a vacant tomb (John 20:4–7). In a culture where women's testimonies were not legally acceptable, Jesus elevated these women's faithfulness, trusting them with his first resurrected encounter and the most astonishing announcement in human history.

The Gospels also addressed the disciples' disbelief and confusion upon hearing the news. Their candid acknowledgment that belief in a resurrected Jesus was not immediate or easy—even for the people closest to him—lent credibility to the Gospel accounts. For the first followers of Jesus, his resurrection confirmed his identity as the Messiah and Son of God, validated his teachings and promises, and transformed a scattered and frightened group of followers into bold witnesses willing to face persecution and even death for their testimony.

Resurrection of Christ, central motive of fresco vault, Michel Corneille the Elder, ca. 1640–1650. Church Saint-Nicolas-des-Champs, Paris, France.

Jesus's miraculous resurrection stands as the event upon which Christianity ultimately depends. This dramatic moment was not just the beginning of the Resurrection narrative—it was the spark of a movement that would reach to the ends of the earth. While all four Gospels emphasized different perspectives and moments of Jesus's resurrection, they were all united in one central claim: Jesus was no longer in the tomb; he had risen from the dead.

From the beginning, Jesus's crucifixion and subsequent resurrection have been prompting controversy and conspiracy theories. Matthew's Gospel recorded that when the Roman guards reported what had happened at the garden tomb, they were told to say that Jesus's disciples stole his body. There have been numerous theories and narratives ever since.

Historically, the Gospel accounts have sparked everything including anti-Semitic attitudes, blaming Jews for the death of Jesus; respect for the Jewish tradition to which Jesus belonged; skepticism due to tensions between the accounts; complete disinterest; and fierce belief that the various Gospel perspectives are parts of the whole. No matter the controversy, the fact remains these stories shaped the next 2,000 years of history. The Western world would be markedly different today if they had not been passed down through the Bible.

SAID JESUS UNTO THEM,
BE NOT AFRAID:
GO TELL MY BRETHREN THAT
THEY GO INTO GALILEE,
AND THERE SHALL THEY
SEE ME.

MATTHEW 28:10, KJV

The Great Commission

Matthew 28:16–20

Sketch for the Church of Saint Francis Xavier: The Mission of the Apostles, Romain Cazes, 1868. Petit Palais, Paris, France.

GO AND MAKE DISCIPLES
OF ALL NATIONS,
BAPTIZING THEM IN
THE NAME OF THE FATHER
AND OF THE SON AND
OF THE HOLY SPIRIT,
AND TEACHING THEM
TO OBEY EVERYTHING I HAVE
COMMANDED YOU.

MATTHEW 28:19–20a, NIV

Many people saw Jesus after his return to life. Luke recorded that the very day of Jesus's resurrection, two of his followers were walking from Jerusalem to Emmaus, a village about seven miles away (Luke 24:13–35). Their conversation was heavy as they tried to make sense of the preceding days. As they walked, a stranger joined them. Unrecognized, it was Jesus himself.

Jesus began interpreting Scriptures for them—how the Messiah must suffer before entering glory. When they reached Emmaus, the two followers of Jesus urged their companion to stay for the evening. At supper, Jesus took bread, blessed and broke it, and gave it to them. In that moment, they recognized him, but he immediately vanished from sight.

The two immediately returned to Jerusalem, eager to share their experience. There they discovered Simon Peter had also seen Jesus. In this atmosphere

Supper at Emmaus, Caravaggio, ca. 1601–1602. National Gallery, London, England, UK.

of astonishment, Jesus himself appeared (John 20:19–23). His first words were reassurance: "Peace be unto you" (KJV). He then invited everyone to touch him, to examine his hands and feet, because the crucifixion wounds were visible. Jesus even asked for food and ate in their presence to underscore the real, embodied nature of his resurrection. He wasn't merely a spiritual vision or symbolic event—he was truly alive.

John recorded that Jesus appeared separately to Thomas, who was skeptical even of his fellow disciples' reports (John 20:24–29). Jesus's willingness to offer tangible proof that he was no apparition but a fully, physically resurrected being, addressed not only the disciples' doubts, but also the doubts of every person who would hear about him throughout history.

Although the religious leaders at the time actively spread a narrative that Jesus's disciples had stolen his body, first-century Christian writings stated that more than 500 people saw Jesus alive (1 Corinthians 15:6), and Luke recorded that Jesus interacted with followers over 40 days' time (Acts 1:3).

Matthew's account of the period after Jesus's return to life was more succinct. On a mountain in Galilee, the resurrected Jesus met with his disciples; some worshipped Jesus immediately, while others doubted—an honest and relatable reflection of human nature in the presence of divine mystery.

Doubting Saint Thomas, Silvestro Lega, 1850. The Modern and Contemporary Civic Gallery, Latina, Italy.

It was in this setting that Jesus gave his disciples their ultimate purpose—make disciples of all nations. Not only were they to continue his work, but they must expand it to the world. His final directive broadened the reach of the Gospel beyond any single group, culture, geography, or generation. Their mission was not only about conversion but *formation*—teaching people to live in alignment with the life and values of Jesus. And he anchored his commission in relationship, assuring the disciples they would be accompanied by the very person who overcame death: himself.

Jesus's Great Commission united his resurrection with the disciples' mission. Rather than ending the story—it launched it. The message of the kingdom of God that began in Galilee with a single man would ultimately travel through Jerusalem, Samaria, to the ends of the earth carried by ordinary people empowered by an extraordinary message.

SURELY I AM
WITH YOU ALWAYS,
TO THE VERY END OF THE AGE.

MATTHEW 28:20b, NIV

IMAGE INDEX

THE ANNUNCIATION

2 *Annunciation*, Leonardo da Vinci, ca. 1472–1475. Uffizi Gallery, Florence, Italy. Public domain. https://commons.wikimedia.org/wiki/File:Leonardo_da_Vinci_-_Annunciazione_-_Google_Art_Project.jpg.

5 *The Archangel Gabriel*, Masolino da Panicale, ca. 1430. National Gallery of Art, Washington, DC, USA. Samuel H. Kress Collection. Used with permission. https://www.nga.gov/artworks/366-archangel-gabriel.

6 *The Prophecy of Isaiah*, Francisco Bayeu, ca. 1778–1779. Museo Nacional del Prado, Madrid, Spain. Permission pending. https://www.museodelprado.es/en/the-collection/art-work/the-prophecy-of-isaiah/5af6e866-307f-4b82-bd2e-7ad5afdb955f.

BIRTH OF JESUS

8 *On the Eve of the Birth of Christ*, Michael Rieser, 1869. Public domain. https://commons.wikimedia.org/wiki/File:Michael_Rieser_Am_Abend_vor_Christi_Geburt_1869.jpg.

11 *Adoration of the Child*, Gerard van Honthorst, ca. 1620. Uffizi Gallery, Florence, Italy. Public domain. https://commons.wikimedia.org/wiki/File:Gerard_van_Honthorst_-_Adoration_of_the_Child_-_WGA11655.jpg.

12 *Adoration of the Shepherds*, Giorgione, ca. 1505–1510. National Gallery of Art, Washington, DC, USA. Public domain. https://commons.wikimedia.org/wiki/File:Giorgione_-_Adoration_of_the_Shepherds_-_National_Gallery_of_Art.jpg.

VISIT OF THE MAGI

14 *The Adoration of the Magi*, Edward Burne-Jones, 1904. Musée d'Orsay, Paris, France. Public domain. https://commons.wikimedia.org/wiki/File:Edward_Burne-Jones_-_The_Adoration_of_the_Magi_-_Google_Art_Project.jpg.

17 *Boswellia sacra*, from which frankincense, a resinous dried sap, is harvested. Near Salalah, Oman. Photo credit: alexeys, 2016. Permission pending. https://www.istockphoto.com/photo/frankincense-tree-gm624959400-109960771?searchscope=image%2Cfilm.

18 *Flight into Egypt*, Eugène Girardet, ca. 1853–1907. Public domain. https://commons.wikimedia.org/wiki/File:Eugène_Girardet,_Flight_into_Egypt.jpg.

PRESENTATION IN THE TEMPLE

20 *The Presentation in the Temple*, Alvaro Pirez, ca. 1405–1415. The Met Fifth Avenue, New York, New York, USA. The Jack and Belle Linsky Collection, 1982. Public domain. https://www.metmuseum.org/art/collection/search/437298.

23 *Simeon the Righteous*, Alexei Yegorovich Yegorov, ca. 1830–1840. Public domain. https://commons.wikimedia.org/wiki/File:Yegorov-Simeon_the_Righteous.jpg.

24 *The Prophetess Anna*, Rembrandt, 1639. Kunsthistorisches Museum, Vienna, Austria. Public domain. https://commons.wikimedia.org/wiki/File:Rembrandt_Harmensz._van_Rijn_085.jpg.

JESUS IN THE TEMPLE AS A BOY

26 *Jesus Among the Doctors*, Jean-Auguste-Dominique Ingres, 1804. Musée Ingres Bourdelle, Montauban, France. Public domain. https://commons.wikimedia.org/wiki/File:Musée_Ingres-Bourdelle_-_Jésus_parmi_les_docteurs_-_Ingres_-_Joconde06070001450.jpg.

29 *On Return from Jerusalem, It Is Noticed that Jesus Is Lost*, James Tissot, ca. 1886–1894. Brooklyn Museum, Brooklyn, New York, USA. Public domain. https://www.brooklynmuseum.org/objects/13394.

30 *Jesus Found in the Temple*, James Tissot, ca. 1886–1894. Brooklyn Museum, Brooklyn, New York, USA. Public domain. https://commons.wikimedia.org/wiki/File:Brooklyn_Museum_-_Jesus_Found_in_the_Temple_(Jesus_retrouvé_dans_le_temple)_-_James_Tissot_-_overall.jpg.

BAPTISM OF JESUS

32 *The Baptism of Christ*, Joachim Patinir, ca. 1510. Kunsthistorisches Museum, Vienna, Austria. Public domain. https://commons.wikimedia.org/wiki/File:Joachim_Patinir_-_Baptism_of_Christ_-_WGA17089.jpg.

35 *Saint John the Baptist*, Juan Martínez Montañés, ca. 1620–1630. Polychromed wood sculpture with gilding. Metropolitan Museum of Art, New York, New York, USA. Purchase, Joseph Pulitzer Bequest, 1963. Public domain. https://commons.wikimedia.org/wiki/File:Saint_John_the_Baptist_MET_DP249462.jpg.

36 *The Baptism of Christ*, Grigory Gagarin, ca. 1840–1850. Russian State Library, Moscow, Russia. Public domain. https://commons.wikimedia.org/wiki/File:Gagarin_KreschenieHristovo.jpg.

TEMPTATION IN THE WILDERNESS

40 *Christ in the Wilderness*, Ivan Kramskoi, 1872. State Tretyakov Gallery, Moscow, Russia. Public domain. https://commons.wikimedia.org/wiki/File:Christ_in_the_Wilderness_-_Ivan_Kramskoy_-_Google_Cultural_Institute.jpg.

43 *The Spirit then Driveth Jesus into the Wilderness*, William Hole, ca. 1906. Library of Congress Prints and Photographs Division, Washington, DC, USA. Credit: G. Eric and Edith Matson Photograph Collection. Public domain. https://commons.wikimedia.org/wiki/File:Matt._4.1._The_spirit_then_driveth_Jesus_into_the_wilderness_LOC_matpc.23116.jpg.

44 *The Temptation of Christ*, Ary Scheffer, 1854. Walker Art Gallery, Liverpool, England, UK. Public domain. https://commons.wikimedia.org/wiki/File:Ary_Scheffer_-_The_Temptation_of_Christ_(1854).jpg.

CALLING THE FIRST DISCIPLES

46 *The Calling of the Apostles Peter and Andrew*, small panel of the Maestà, Duccio di Buoninsegna, ca. 1308–1311. National Gallery of Art, Washington, DC, USA. Credit: Samuel H. Kress Collection. Public domain. https://commons.wikimedia.org/wiki/File:Duccio_di_Buoninsegna_036.jpg.

49 *The Calling of Andrew and Simon Peter*, possibly a left wing of an altarpiece, follower of Rogier van der Weyden, ca. 1440. Upton House, Warwickshire, England, UK. Credit: Upton House, The Bearsted Collection (National Trust). Public domain. https://commons.wikimedia.org/wiki/File:Rogier_van_der_Weyden_(c.1399-1464)_(follower_of)_-_The_Calling_of_Saint_Andrew_and_Another_Disciple_of_Saint_John_the_Baptist_-_446747_-_National_Trust.jpg.

50 *The Calling of Saint Matthew*, copy after Jan Sanders van Hemessen, early 1600s. Metropolitan Museum of Art, New York, New York, USA. Public domain. https://commons.wikimedia.org/wiki/File:The_Calling_of_Matthew_MET_DT201070.jpg.

WEDDING AT CANA

52 *The Wedding at Cana*, Paolo Caliari, known as Veronese, 1562–1563. Musée du Louvre, Paris, France. Public domain. https://commons.wikimedia.org/wiki/File:Paolo_Veronese,_The_Wedding_at_Cana.JPG.

55 *Marriage at Cana*, fresco by unknown artist, ca. 1350. Visoki Dečani Monastery, Deçan, Kosovo. Used with permission. https://commons.wikimedia.org/wiki/File:Marriage_at_Cana-Decani-monastery-small.jpg.

56 *Marriage at Cana* (detail), fresco in Cycle of the Life of the Christ, middle tier north wall, Giotto, 1304–1306. Scrovegni Chapel, Padua, Veneto, Italy. Public domain. https://commons.wikimedia.org/wiki/File:Giotto_di_Bondone_-_No._24_Scenes_from_the_Life_of_Christ_-_8._Marriage_at_Cana_(detail)_-_WGA09203.jpg.

JESUS PROCLAIMS HIS PURPOSE

58 *Indiction*, fresco by unknown artist, ca. 1350. Visoki Dečani Monastery, Deçan, Kosovo. https://russianicons.wordpress.com/tag/jesus/.

61 A scroll of the book of Isaiah. Photo credit: Pete Unseth, 2009. Public domain. https://commons.wikimedia.org/wiki/File:Isaiah_scroll.PNG.

62 *The Brow of the Hill Near Nazareth*, James Tissot, ca. 1886–1894. Brooklyn Museum, Brooklyn, New York, USA. Public domain. https://commons.wikimedia.org/wiki/File:Brooklyn_Museum_-_The_Brow_of_the_Hill_near_Nazareth_(L%27escarpement_de_Nazareth)_-_James_Tissot.jpg.

THE BEATITUDES

64 *Sermon on the Mountain*, Károly Ferenczy, 1896. Magyar Nemzeti Galéria, Budapest, Hungary. Photo credit: Yelkrokoyade. Used with permission. https://commons.wikimedia.org/wiki/File:The_Sermon_on_the_Mount_Károly_Ferenczy.jpg.

67 "The Eight Beatitudes," folio from Walters manuscript W.171, Dirc van Delf, ca. 1400–1404. Walters Art Museum, Baltimore, MD, USA. Public domain. https://commons.wikimedia.org/wiki/File:Dirc_van_Delft_-_The_Eight_Beatitudes_-_Walters_W17160V_-_Full_Page.jpg.

68 *Jesus Preaching on the Mountain*, Gustave Doré, 1865–1868. Location unknown. Public domain. https://freechristimages.com/images-Christ-life/Jesus-Preaching-Sermon-on-the-Mount_-Gustave-Dore.jpg.

THE LORD'S PRAYER

70 *Sermon on the Mount*, Fritz von Uhde, ca. 1877. Museum of Fine Arts, Budapest, Hungary. Public domain. https://commons.wikimedia.org/wiki/File:Fritz_von_Uhde_Bergpredigt.jpg.

73 "The Lord's Prayer," from *The Sermon on the Mount*, Folio 17-18, Owen Carter Jones, published by Longman & Co., 1845. Public domain. https://commons.wikimedia.org/wiki/File:The_Sermon_on_the_Mount_(Owen_Jones;_pp._17-18).jpg.

74 Ibid.

PARABLE OF THE SOWER

78 *The Sower*, Vincent van Gogh, 1888. Kröller-Müller Museum, Otterlo, Netherlands. Used with permission. https://commons.wikimedia.org/wiki/File:Sower_at_Sunset_-_Vincent_Van_Gogh.jpg.

81 *Parable of the Sower*, Antonios Fikos, 2012. Used with permission. https://commons.wikimedia.org/wiki/File:The_parable_of_the_sower.jpg.

82 *Christ of the Cornfield*, Kuzma Petrov-Vodkin, 1914. Location unknown. Public domain. https://commons.wikimedia.org/wiki/File:Christ_of_the_Cornfield_by_Petrov-Vodkin.jpg.

PARABLE OF THE GOOD SAMARITAN

84 *The Good Samaritan*, Maximilien Luce, 1896. Private collection. Photo credit: Christie's. Public domain. https://commons.wikimedia.org/wiki/File:Maximilien_Luce_-_Le_bon_samaritain.jpg.

87 *The Good Samaritan*, George Frederic Watts, 1850. Manchester Art Gallery, Manchester, England, UK. Public domain. https://commons.wikimedia.org/wiki/File:George_Frederic_Watts_(1817-1904)_-_The_Good_Samaritan_-_1882.149_-_Manchester_Art_Gallery.jpg.

88 *The Parable of the Good Samaritan*, Edward Carter Preston, 1921. Memorial window to the parents of Selwyn Lloyd, MP, Speaker of the House of Commons, north aisle of West Kirby Methodist Church, West Kirby, Merseyside, England, UK. Photo credit: Phil Nash. Used with permission. https://commons.wikimedia.org/wiki/File:Lloyd_window,_West_Kirby_Methodist_Church.jpg.

PARABLE OF THE PRODIGAL SON

90 *The Departure of the Prodigal Son*, Bartolomé Esteban Murillo, 1660s. National Gallery of Ireland, Dublin, Ireland. Public domain. https://commons.wikimedia.org/wiki/File:Murillo_-_The_Prodigal_Son_Restored.jpg.

93 *The Prodigal Son*, Jacob Jordaens, 1640. Gemäldegalerie Alte Meister, Dresden, Germany. Used with permission. https://commons.wikimedia.org/wiki/File:Dresden,_Gemäldegalerie_Alte_Meister,_Jacob_Jordaens,_der_verlorene_Sohn.jpg.

94 *The Return of the Prodigal Son, Father*, Andrei Mironov, 2023. Ryazan, Russia. Used with permission. https://commons.wikimedia.org/wiki/File:Return_of_the_prodigal_son._Father._A._Mironov.jpg.

PARABLE OF THE MUSTARD SEED

96 *Jesus and the Parable of the Mustard Seed* icon, unknown. Public domain. https://commons.wikimedia.org/wiki/File:Jesus_and_the_parable_of_the_mustard_seed.jpg.

99 Illustration of *brassica nigra*, Walther Otto Müller, 1897. Public domain. https://commons.wikimedia.org/wiki/File:Brassica_nigra_-_Köhler–s_Medizinal-Pflanzen-170.jpg.

100 Mustard trees, National Park Service photographer, 2025. Santa Monica Mountains National Recreation Area, California, USA. Public domain. https://commons.wikimedia.org/wiki/File:Mustard_Seed_(9096494409).jpg.

101 Illustration of European goldfinch, unknown artist, *Birds and Nature Vol. XIII*, A. W. Mumford Publisher, 1903. Smithsonian Libraries, Washington, DC, USA. https://commons.wikimedia.org/wiki/File:Birds_and_nature_(1903)_(14564039058).jpg.

JESUS AND THE CHILDREN

102 *Christ Among Children*, Henryk Siemiradzki, 1872. National Museum in Warsaw, Warsaw, Poland. Public domain. https://commons.wikimedia.org/wiki/File:Henryk_Siemiradzki_-_Christ_among_children_-_MP_1025_MNW_-_National_Museum_in_Warsaw.jpg.

105 *Suffer the Children*, Carl Bloch, ca. 1865–1879. Chapel at Frederiksborg Palace, Copenhagen, Denmark. Public domain. https://commons.wikimedia.org/wiki/File:Carl_Heinrich_Bloch_-_Suffer_the_Children.jpg.

106 *Christ Receiving the Children*, Sébastien Bourdon, 1655. Art Institute of Chicago, Chicago, Illinois, USA. Public domain. https://commons.wikimedia.org/wiki/File:Christ_Receiving_the_Children.jpg.

THE GREATEST COMMANDMENT

108 *The Pharisees and the Sadducees Come to Tempt Jesus*, James Tissot, ca. 1886–1894. Brooklyn Museum, Brooklyn, New York, USA. Public domain. https://www.brooklynmuseum.org/objects/4515.

111 *The Nash Papyrus* contains a portion of a pre-Masoretic Text, specifically the Ten Commandments and the *Shema Yisrael* prayer, ca. 100s BC. Proceedings of the Society of Biblical Archæology, Volume 25 (January-December 1903), 56. Public domain. https://commons.wikimedia.org/wiki/File:2nd_century_Hebrew_decalogue.jpg.

112 *Christ Among the Pharisees*, Jacob Jordaens, ca. 1660–1670. Private collection. Public domain. https://commons.wikimedia.org/wiki/File:Christ_among_the_Pharisees.jpg.

CALMING THE STORM

116 *Christ in the Storm on the Sea of Galilee*, Ludolf Bakhuizen, 1695. Indianapolis Museum of Art, Indianapolis, Indiana, USA. Public domain. https://commons.wikimedia.org/wiki/File:Backhuysen,_Ludolf,_I_-_Christ_in_the_Storm_on_the_Sea_of_Galilee_-_Google_Art_Project.jpg.

119 "Reference Map of Ancient Palestine" (detail of Galilee), from *The Historical Atlas*, Folio 6-7, William R. Shepherd, published by Henry Holt and Company, 1911. Public domain. https://commons.wikimedia.org/wiki/File:Ancient_Galilee.jpg.

120 *Jesus on the Lake of Gennesaret*, Alexandre-Gabriel Decamps, ca. 1850–1875. Louvre Museum, Paris, France. Public domain. https://commons.wikimedia.org/wiki/File:Jésus_sur_le_lac_de_Génésareth_-_Alexandre-Gabriel_Decamps_-_Musée_du_Louvre_Peintures_RF_1648.jpg.

FEEDING THE 5,000

122 *Feeding the Five Thousand*, John Martin, ca. 1789–1854. Yale Center for British Art, New Haven, Connecticut, USA. Credit: Yale Center for British Art, Paul Mellon Collection. Public domain. https://commons.wikimedia.org/wiki/File:John_Martin_-_Feeding_the_Five_Thousand_-_B1977.14.4260_-_Yale_Center_for_British_Art.jpg.

125 *Hills of Galilee*, John Singer Sargent, 1905–1906. Brooklyn Museum, Brooklyn, New York, USA. Public domain. https://commons.wikimedia.org/wiki/File:Brooklyn_Museum_-_Hills_of_Galilee_-_John_Singer_Sargent.jpg.

126 Mosaic tile floor depicting loaves and fishes at the reported site of Jesus feeding 5,000, unknown artist, ca. AD 480. Church of the Multiplication, Tabgha, Israel. Photo credit: Croberto68, 2009. Public domain. https://commons.wikimedia.org/wiki/File:Tabgha_-_Church_of_the_Multiplication_3.jpg.

WALKING ON WATER

128 *Man of Sorrows*, William Dyce, ca. 1860. National Galleries of Scotland, Edinburgh, Scotland, UK. Public domain. https://commons.wikimedia.org/wiki/File:Man_of_Sorrows,_by_William_Dyce.jpg.

131 *The Disciples See Christ Walking on the Water*, Henry Ossawa Tanner, 1907. Des Moines Art Center, Des Moines, Iowa, USA. Public domain. https://commons.wikimedia.org/wiki/File:Henry_Ossawa_Tanner,_The_Disciples_See_Christ_Walking_on_the_Water,_c._1907.jpg.

132 *Christ at the Sea of Galilee*, likely Lambert Sustris, ca. 1570–1575. National Gallery of Art, Washington, DC, USA. Credit: Samuel H. Kress Collection. Public domain. https://commons.wikimedia.org/wiki/File:Tintoretto,_Jacopo_-_Christ_at_the_Sea_of_Galilee.jpg.

HEALING THE PHYSICALLY ILL WOMAN

134 *Christ Healing the Blind*, Philippe de Champaigne, ca. 1655–1660. Timken Museum of Art, San Diego, California, USA. Public domain. https://commons.wikimedia.org/wiki/File:Christ_Healing_the_Blind_by_Philippe_de_Champaigne,_Timken_Museum_of_Art.JPG.

137 *Mark 5:22-34. On the Way to the House of Jairus*, William Hole, 1846–1917. Library of Congress, Washington, DC, USA. Credit: G. Eric and Edith Matson Photograph Collection. Public domain. https://commons.wikimedia.org/wiki/File:Mark_5-22-34._On_the_way_to_the_house_of_Jairus,_whose_little_daughter_lieth_sick,_He_healeth_a_woman_in_the_crowd,_and_commendeth_her_faith_LOC_matpc.23125.jpg.

138 *The Healing of a Bleeding Woman*, fresco by unknown artist, ca. AD 301–400. Catacombs of Marcellinus and Peter, Rome, Italy. Photo credit: Grabar, The Art of Early Christianity, 2009. Public domain. https://commons.wikimedia.org/wiki/File:Healing_of_a_bleeding_women_Marcellinus-Peter-Catacomb.jpg.

CASTING OUT DEMONS

140 *The Conversion of Mary Magdalene*, Paolo Veronese, ca. 1548. National Gallery, London, England, UK. Public domain. https://commons.wikimedia.org/wiki/File:Paolo_Veronese,_The_Conversion_of_Mary_Magdalene.jpg.

143 *Christ Healing a Lunatic and Judas Receiving Thirty Pieces of Silver*, Francesco d'Antonio di Bartolomeo, ca. 1425–1426. Philadelphia Museum of Art, Philadelphia, Pennsylvania, USA. Photo credit: Maltaper, 2023. Used with permission. https://commons.wikimedia.org/wiki/File:Francesco_d%27Antonio_-_Christ_Healing_a_Lunatic_and_Judas_Receiving_Thirty_Pieces_of_Silver.jpg.

144 "The Exorcism," from *Très Riches Heures du duc de Berry*, Folio 166r, Limbourg Brothers, ca. 1412–1416. Condé Museum, Chantilly, France. Public domain. https://commons.wikimedia.org/wiki/File:Folio_166r_-_The_Exorcism.jpg.

RAISING PEOPLE FROM THE DEAD

146 *The Raising of Jairus's Daughter*, George Percy Jacomb-Hood, 1895. Guildhall Art Gallery, London, England, UK. Public domain. https://commons.wikimedia.org/wiki/File:George_Percy_Jacomb-Hood_-_The_Raising_of_Jairus%27_Daughter_(1895).jpg.

149 "Jesus Raises a Widow's Son at Nain," from illuminated and illustrated Arabic *Gospels* created in Egypt, Folio 157A, Ilyas Basim Khuri Bazzi Rahib, 1684. Walters Art Museum, Baltimore, Maryland, USA. Credit: Acquired by Henry Walters. Public domain. https://commons.wikimedia.org/wiki/File:Ilyas_Basim_Khuri_Bazzi_Rahib_-_Jesus_Raises_a_Widow%3Fs_Son_at_Nain_-_Walters_W592157A_-_Full_Page.jpg.

150 *The Raising of Lazarus (after Rembrandt)*, Vincent van Gogh, 1890. Van Gogh Museum, Amsterdam, Netherlands. Photo credit: GoldenArtists, 2023. Used with permission. https://commons.wikimedia.org/wiki/File:The_Raising_of_Lazarus_-_Vincent_Van_Gogh.jpg.

JESUS'S TRIUMPHAL ENTRY

154 *Entry of the Christ in Jerusalem*, Jean-Léon Gérôme, 1897. Musée Georges-Garret, Vesoul, France. Public domain. https://commons.wikimedia.org/wiki/File:Gérôme_-_L%27entrée_du_Christ_à_Jérusalem_-_cadre.jpg.

157 *Christ's Entry into Jerusalem*, fresco in southern transept of Lower Basilica, Pietro Lorenzetti, ca. 1310–1329. Basilica of Saint Francis of Assisi, Assisi, Italy. Public domain. https://commons.wikimedia.org/wiki/File:Assisi-frescoes-entry-into-jerusalem-pietro_lorenzetti.jpg.

158 *Reconstruction of Jerusalem and the Temple of Herod*, James Tissot, ca. 1886–1894. Brooklyn Museum, Brooklyn, New York, USA. Public domain. https://www.brooklynmuseum.org/objects/13389.

THE LAST SUPPER

160 *The Last Supper*, fresco, Leonardo da Vinci, 1495–1498. Santa Maria delle Grazie, Milan, Italy. Photo credit: Binarystring, 2013. Used with permission. https://commons.wikimedia.org/wiki/File:The_Last_Supper_-_Leonardo_Da_Vinci_-_High_Resolution_32x16.jpg.

163 *Christ Washing the Feet of His Disciples*, Jacopo Tintoretto, ca. 1547. Museo del Prado, Madrid, Spain. Public domain. https://commons.wikimedia.org/wiki/File:El_Lavatorio_(Tintoretto).jpg.

164 *The Last Supper*, Pieter Pourbus, 1548. Groeninge Museum, Bruges, Belgium. Photo credit: Vassil, 2016. Used with permission. https://commons.wikimedia.org/wiki/File:Groeningemuseum_Pieter_Pourbus_Last_Supper_01052015_2.jpg.

THE CRUCIFIXION

166 *Christ Carrying the Cross*, Titian, 1565. Museo del Prado, Madrid, Spain. Public domain. https://commons.wikimedia.org/wiki/File:Titian,_Christ_Carrying_the_Cross._Oil_on_canvas,_67_x_77_cm,_c._1565._Madrid,_Museo_Nacional_del_Prado.jpg.

169 *Night at Golgotha*, Vasily Petrovich Vereshchagin, 1869. State Tretyakov Gallery, Moscow, Russia. Public domain. https://commons.wikimedia.org/wiki/File:Ночь_на_Голгофе.jpg.

170 *The Crucifixion* (detail, soldier on horseback), unknown Netherlandish artist, ca. 1520. Gemäldegalerie, Berlin, Germany. Photo credit: Warburg, 2013. Used with permission. https://commons.wikimedia.org/wiki/File:Crucifixion_nl_soldier.jpg.

JESUS'S BURIAL

172 *The Descent from the Cross*, Rogier van der Weyden, ca. 1435–1438. Museo del Prado, Madrid, Spain. Public domain. https://commons.wikimedia.org/wiki/File:El_Descendimiento,_by_Rogier_van_der_Weyden,_from_Prado_in_Google_Earth.jpg.

175 *Pietà du Château d'Ecouen*, Rosso Fiorentino, 1537–1540. Louvre Museum, Paris, France. Photo credit: Philippel, 2016. Used with permission. https://commons.wikimedia.org/wiki/File:Pietà_du_Château_d%27Ecouen.jpg.

176 *Sketch for the Chapel of the Sorbonne: Christ in the Tomb*, Louis Charles Timbal, 1870–1875. Petit Palais, Paris, France. Photo credit: Pierre Yves Beaudouin, 2020. Used with permission. https://commons.wikimedia.org/wiki/File:Louis_Charles_Timbal_-_Esquisse_pour_la_chapelle_de_la_Sorbonne_-_Le_Christ_au_tombeau_-_PPP4802_-_Musée_des_Beaux-Arts_de_la_ville_de_Paris_-_2.jpg.

THE RESURRECTION OF JESUS

178 *An Angel Opens the Grave of Christ*, Benjamin Gerritszoon Cuyp, ca. 1630–1649. Dordrechts Museum, Dordrecht, Netherlands. Public domain. https://commons.wikimedia.org/wiki/File:Benjamin_Gerritsz._Cuyp_-_De_engel_bij_het_graf_-_NK2107_-_Cultural_Heritage_Agency_of_the_Netherlands_Art_Collection.jpg.

181 *The Three Women on the Tomb of Christ*, Irma Martin, 1843. Private collection. Photo credit: BeatrixBelibaste, 2020. Public domain. https://commons.wikimedia.org/wiki/File:Irma_Martin_-_The_three_women_on_the_tomb_of_Christ.jpg.

182 *Resurrection of Christ*, central motive of fresco vault, Michel Corneille the Elder, ca. 1640–1650. Church Saint-Nicolas-des-Champs, Paris, France. Photo credit: Jebulon, 2011. Used with permission. https://commons.wikimedia.org/wiki/File:Résurrection_Corneille_cartouche_central_2.jpg.

THE GREAT COMMISSION

184 *Sketch for the Church of Saint Francis Xavier: The Mission of the Apostles*, Romain Cazes, 1868. Petit Palais, Paris, France. Photo credit: Pierre Yves Beaudouin, 2020. Used with permission. https://commons.wikimedia.org/wiki/File:Romain_Cazes_-_Esquisse_pour_l%27église_Saint-François-Xavier_-_La_mission_des_Apôtres_-_PPP4535_-_Musée_des_Beaux-Arts_de_la_ville_de_Paris_-_2.jpg.

187 *Supper at Emmaus*, Caravaggio, ca. 1601–1602. National Gallery, London, England, UK. Photo credit: Adrian Pingstone, 2003. Public domain. https://commons.wikimedia.org/wiki/File:Caravaggio.emmaus.750pix.jpg.

188 *Doubting Saint Thomas*, Silvestro Lega, 1850. The Modern and Contemporary Civic Gallery, Latina, Italy. Public domain. https://commons.wikimedia.org/wiki/File:Doubting_Saint_Thomas_(1850)_-_Silvestro_Lega.jpg.

About the Author

Jerry Pattengale, PhD, is a founding scholar at the Museum of the Bible in Washington, DC where he still serves as Senior Advisor, and a distinguished professor and administrator at Indiana Wesleyan University (IWU). His influence also extends beyond academia. As a Senior Fellow with the Sagamore Institute, CSR associate publisher, JEC board member at Yale Divinity School, and a member of the National Press Club's Membership Committee, he continues to shape thought leadership on history, faith, and culture at the state and global levels.

Dr. Pattengale has authored dozens of books and hundreds of articles and columns, including in prominent publications like the *Chicago Tribune*, *Washington Post*, and *The Wall Street Journal*. His recent works, *The New Book of Christian Martyrs* (Tyndale House, 2023); *The Anxious Middle* (Baylor University Press, 2023); *The World's Greatest Book*, 2nd ed. (Tyndale House, 2023); and *Habits of Hope* (IVP, 2024) have received critical acclaim. He is known for his award-winning "Buck Creek" newsprint series for its engaging and insightful storytelling. His *Inexplicable* TV series, hosted by Dennis Haysbert, also won three Telly Awards.

Born and raised in Buck Creek, Indiana, Dr. Pattengale's journey from poverty and homelessness at the end of high school to becoming a globally recognized scholar is an inspiration. He even addressed the United Nations, attended meetings at the White House, and was interim president of Religion News Service. With the support of church members and alumni of Marion College (now IWU), he pursued higher education, serving as student body president and recognized as the outstanding graduate. Dr. Pattengale went on to earn Master's degrees at Wheaton (IL) and Miami University (Ohio). He then earned his PhD at Miami University under the eminent historian, Edwin M. Yamauchi, with perfect marks and established himself as an active voice in his field.